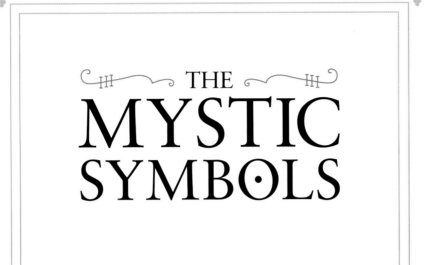

THE
MYSTIC
SYMBOLS

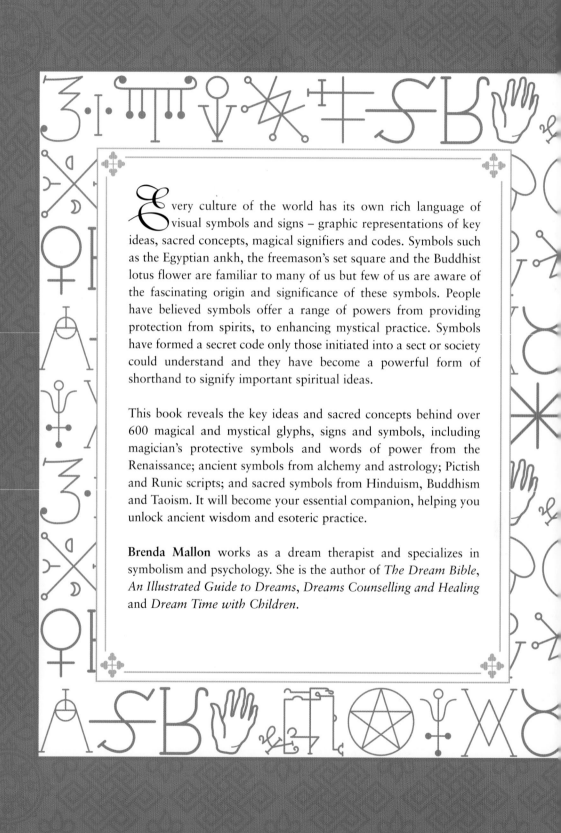

*E*very culture of the world has its own rich language of visual symbols and signs – graphic representations of key ideas, sacred concepts, magical signifiers and codes. Symbols such as the Egyptian ankh, the freemason's set square and the Buddhist lotus flower are familiar to many of us but few of us are aware of the fascinating origin and significance of these symbols. People have believed symbols offer a range of powers from providing protection from spirits, to enhancing mystical practice. Symbols have formed a secret code only those initiated into a sect or society could understand and they have become a powerful form of shorthand to signify important spiritual ideas.

This book reveals the key ideas and sacred concepts behind over 600 magical and mystical glyphs, signs and symbols, including magician's protective symbols and words of power from the Renaissance; ancient symbols from alchemy and astrology; Pictish and Runic scripts; and sacred symbols from Hinduism, Buddhism and Taoism. It will become your essential companion, helping you unlock ancient wisdom and esoteric practice.

Brenda Mallon works as a dream therapist and specializes in symbolism and psychology. She is the author of *The Dream Bible, An Illustrated Guide to Dreams, Dreams Counselling and Healing* and *Dream Time with Children*.

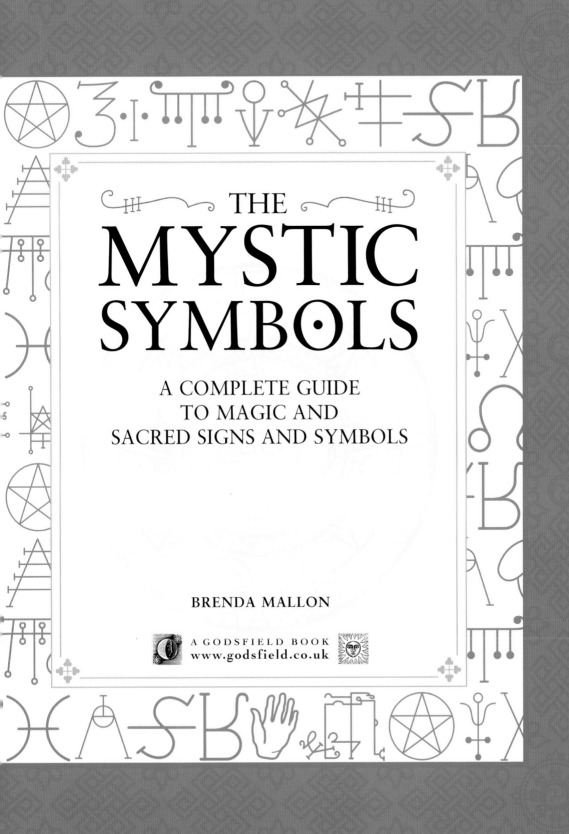

THE
MYSTIC
SYMBOLS

A COMPLETE GUIDE
TO MAGIC AND
SACRED SIGNS AND SYMBOLS

BRENDA MALLON

A GODSFIELD BOOK
www.godsfield.co.uk

An Hachette Livre UK Company

First published in Great Britain in 2007
by Godsfield Press,
a division of
Octopus Publishing Group Ltd
2–4 Heron Quays,
London E14 4JP

Brenda Mallon asserts the moral right to
be identified as the author of this work.

ISBN-13: 978-1-841-81318-9
ISBN-10: 1-841-81318-4

A CIP catalogue record for this book
is available from the British Library

Printed and bound in China

1 3 5 7 9 10 8 6 4 2

The ancient symbols in this book have evolved
over centuries and controversy continues
regarding precise details and interpretation.
This book aims to present the most thoroughly
researched depiction and meaning possible, based
on ancient artworks and manuscripts, but inevitably
other depictions and interpretations will exist.
Ultimately, the power of symbols goes beyond
simple representation and relates to each
individual's own consciousness.

ONTENTS

$\mathscr{O}$INTRODUCTION

Man is a symbolizing animal – wherever humans have been on our planet, they have always used and created symbols. In fact, it seems we cannot do without them. Symbols have a power beyond words because they carry a multitude of meanings that speak to the soul, the mind and the emotions. Symbols challenge us to go beyond what stares us in the face, to go beyond the obvious. So, what is a symbol?

A symbol is different from a sign. A sign points the way, whereas a symbol always stands for something more than its immediate meaning. The potential significance of a symbol is far greater than it appears at first glance. A symbol represents an abstract idea or concept, which may not easily be put into words.

The symbols in this book are based on visual references from ancient manuscripts, artworks and sculptures. There is uncertainty and controversy over the meaning and interpretation of some of the symbols so this book aims to reflect the most commonly held view.

Some symbols have been used by many cultures and societies throughout the ages, often to signify similar concepts, but their longevity and prevalence mean that they have been modified, or that slightly different versions of them exist. Again, this book aims to reflect the most significant elements of any symbol and the most common depiction of it.

Many ancient civilizations used glyphs, or picture symbols, to represent an object or concept. Glyphs tend to be more graphic than symbols and less prone to varying depictions and interpretations.

Many of the symbols we see around us today were created by the earliest civilizations. Many were concerned with the movement of the Sun and Moon and the solar system, and included symbols for the seasons and the gods who governed them. The symbols used in religious tradition and modern magic have a common ancestry that takes us back to a time before writing was invented. They are so powerful because they are archetypal symbols.

The word 'archetype' derives from the Greek compound *arche* and *tupos*: *arche* means the beginning or the first principle of the world, the original creative force; and *tupos* means an imprint or impression, a manifestation of that unseen creative force. Carl Jung says that these archetypal symbols are inherited from our earliest ancestors and that our collective unconscious, or inborn ways of perceiving the world, allow us to know and respond to symbols without necessarily thinking about them. They exert a powerful influence, which is why, by understanding the secret system behind the symbols, we can have more awareness and power in our own lives.

The world of symbolism is a dynamic one. It expands as knowledge and customs change, yet symbols retain kernels of universal wisdom to which humans throughout the millennia have responded and continue to respond. They appear in myths, legends, mystical traditions, art and literature. Wherever we are, we are wrapped in symbols.

The language of the unconscious is the language of symbols. Symbols are the language of the occult in its purest sense; they reveal that which is hidden, expressing an inner reality of which we are often unaware, though mankind has been in touch with this since the earliest times. In the cave paintings of Lascaux in France and in the Aboriginal paintings in Australia, it is clear that the images reflect a deep connection to the natural world, the cosmos and sympathetic magical beliefs. As paintings and carvings developed over the Paleolithic period they symbolized teachings and knowledge available only to those who were initiated into that group. So, we see animals venerated and hunted, and totems to protect the hunter. In our own time, we see symbols of protection in the form of amulet pendants in India and Ireland and in feng shui arrangements in America and England.

In the following chapters you can find the key to the secret world of symbolism and discover where it fits in with ceremonial magic, esoteric societies, religious teachings and sacred practices.

SYMBOLS OF ANCIENT CIVILIZATIONS

Many of the earliest symbols emerged from the rituals and myth-making of ancient civilizations and are still used today. Throughout the ancient world, people sought to understand the mysterious world in which they lived. They developed systems to study the Sun, Moon and stars and constructed cosmologies to explain the universe; in doing so, they identified gods who controlled their destinies, and devised ways to propitiate these deities to escape harm and bring good fortune.

On the following pages we look at symbols that emerged from ancient cultures, including those based in the cradle of civilization between the Tigris and Euphrates rivers – ancient Egypt, Assyria, Babylon, Sumeria and Mesopotamia – which gave rise to cities where laws, systems and cohesion developed. Written language emerged; cuneiform script invented by the ancient Sumerians in the 4th millennium BCE began as a system of pictographs which developed into a series of symbols.

Magic and ritual symbols dominated art and religion in ancient civilizations and each subject had its own unique set of mystical symbols. Pyramids and ziggurats symbolized the primordial mound from which all life arose and many symbols reflected beliefs about creation, life, death and ideas about how the world must be sustained. The Egyptians had an elaborate system of hieroglyphic writing in which 'glyphs' represented both images and sounds yet also held mystic power. Symbols of the Sun, Moon and heavens feature widely, as do variations of the Tree of Life.

Ancient Egypt

The ancient Egyptian civilization flourished for more that 4,000 years and during that time religion and magic merged as a powerful force. Talismans, amulets, pictures and spells were combined with chants, prayers and incantations to protect people from harmful beings and spirits and to win the favour of deities. Egyptian symbols affirmed their ideas, attitudes and concepts regarding life, death and the supernatural. Artists, architects and craftsmen used symbols in the design and construction of temples, in pottery, in tombs and other monuments.

THE PYRAMIDS

The famous Pyramids of Giza reveal the importance of symbols in ancient Egyptian civilization; here we see layer upon layer of symbolism. The pyramids were symbolic stairways to Heaven, which allowed the dead king to ascend from the Earth to his celestial home in the afterlife. The pyramids of the first dynasties were not visibly on display as they are today; once completed, they were covered and hidden by mounds of earth. This burial in the earth symbolized rebirth and resurrection, and the ancient Egyptians equipped the mummy buried within the pyramid with all the items necessary for their journey to the afterlife.

HIEROGLYPHS

Even the ancient Egyptian form of writing was symbolic – hieroglyphs, from the Greek meaning 'sacred carvings', consisted of pictures that had phonetic values. For example, the picture of an owl became the letter 'm', the cobra the letter 'g'. The Egyptians called these hieroglyphs 'the speech of the gods' and believed that the symbols themselves had magical powers. In time, certain hieroglyphs came to be used by them on amulets and talismans as powerful protective symbols.

A WORLD OF OPPOSITES

Many Egyptian symbols are inextricably tied to the landscape and the natural world. The extremes of the physical environment are represented by red for the Sahara Desert and black for the fertile area of the Nile Valley. These opposites formed the basis of the Egyptian world view. Egyptian politics were also symbolized pictorially – for example, the Double Crown symbolized the unification of the kingdoms of Upper and Lower Egypt.

The two ankhs, held by the carved pharoah, symbolize life after death.

ANKH

The ankh is probably the best known of all Egyptian symbols. It was the symbol of all life, both divine and human, and represented the key of knowledge to the mysteries and hidden wisdom. The ankh is associated with the two elements that the Egyptians believed were essential for life – air and water.

In wall paintings and carvings the gods are frequently shown holding an ankh symbol to the nose of a pharaoh or queen, bestowing eternal life through the medium of air. At other times, the ankh is shown with stylized streams of water, energy or small ankhs gushing forth to flow over the pharaoh.

The ankh is also involved in death and funerary rites; when carried by the dead it symbolizes safe passage to the next life, while held upside down it unlocks the gates of death to eternity beyond.

No one knows for certain the origin of the ankh symbol. One theory is that the top loop represents a vagina, and the cross piece and central support symbolize a penis and testicles. Together the loop and crosspiece create the ankh, forming a composite of female and male sexual organs that perform the greatest miracle of all, the creation of new life.

EYE OF HORUS

The Eye of Horus represents soundness or wholeness and appears frequently as an amulet and on wall paintings and carvings. Known as *wadjat*, the Eye of Horus represents the left eye of the falcon-headed god Horus.

Horus's eye was ripped out when he did battle with his evil uncle Set to avenge the murder of his father Osiris. The eye was cast into the sky and came to represent the Moon. Troth, the healing god of the Moon restored the injured eye. The eye took 29 days to heal and the phases of the Moon represented its healing. At the dark of the Moon it is most damaged, with the waxing Moon it heals, until at full Moon it is whole again.

The restorative powers of the Eye of Horus are revealed in the myth of Osiris. Horus offers his healed eye to his dead father and it is so powerful that it helps bring Osiris back to life.

LION

In Egyptian paintings and carvings the lion is depicted as a powerful force, the personification of the Sun and solar power. It represents royal majesty, strength, courage, and their opposites, cruelty and the capacity to bring death. The ancient Egyptians believed the lion oversaw the annual life-giving inundation of the Nile, because the floods coincided with the period when the Sun entered the sign of Leo. Victory over death was symbolized by the wearing of lion skins.

JACKAL

The god Anubis, shown in Egyptian carvings and paintings with the head of a jackal and body of a man, was the god of death as well as its announcer. He was also the guardian of tombs, the god of embalming and the ruler of the Underworld. His role was to comfort, guide and sustain the soul of the deceased until the moment of divine judgement. The jackal was also the protector of the liver and would be invoked to ward off illness.

BULL

The bull Apis was a symbol of fertility and fecundity. It was seen as an avatar, the embodiment of Osiris, Lord of the Underworld, and sacred to the Sun god Ra, the Bull of Heaven, who daily impregnated the sky goddess Nut.

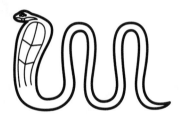

COBRA

The image of the cobra, with its head erect and its hood extended, symbolized the burning eye of Ra, the Sun god. The cobra was known as the eye *uzait*, a symbol of mystic insight and wisdom. In ancient Egypt the *udjats*, or painted eye, represented the all-seeing eyes of Ra and eternity.

Uraeus, a stylized upright form of a spitting cobra, represents the sacred serpent and royal power. Two *uraei* on each side of a winged solar disc were worn on the crown or headdresses of gods and sovereigns and were associated with the Sun and many deities. The Egyptians believed that the cobra would protect the pharaoh by spitting fire at approaching enemies.

HEART

The heart was the only organ left in the body after mummification because it was regarded as the centre of the human being, the place of intelligence and wisdom, and indispensable for life in eternity. The ancient Egyptians believed that the heart of a dead person held the essence of truth.

The 'Weighing of the Heart' was a symbolic ceremony where a panel of gods, including the god Osiris, weighed the heart against the feather of justice. Maat, the goddess of truth and justice and daughter of Ra, held the scales. If the scales balanced, the deceased was given permission to enter the welcoming Underworld; but if the scales tipped under the weight of the heart, it was eaten by a monster.

FETISH

The ancient Egyptians hung animal skins from sticks that symbolized Osiris and Anubis. The fetish represented divine energy that was captured and ready for use whenever it was needed. The magical properties attributed to the animals could be activated by the holder of the stick, usually a shamanistic figure with supernatural powers. Earlier, in the Naqada III era of pre-dynastic Egypt, sacred animals or plants were used as totem, fetish or emblem to represent territorial divisions called *nomes*. The fetish stick or 'standard' represented the spirit of the gods that was invoked to appease them and ensure protection from natural disaster.

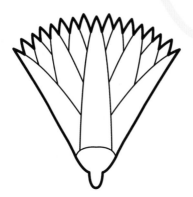

LOTUS

The lotus or Egyptian Blue Lily, which grows along the Nile, was highly significant to ancient Egyptians. It is the symbol of the Sun, of creation and rebirth, since the lotus flower was supposed to close each night and sink beneath the water, then surface again as the Sun rises. In fact, the flower buds rise to the surface over a period of two or three days, open in the morning, then close in the afternoon. The lotus symbolizes royalty and is sacred to Horus, 'He of the lotus', Lord of the Sky; it is also the symbol of Nerfertem, the Egyptian god of healing.

NEBU

This symbol represents gold, which was regarded as a divine metal. Gold was considered to be the flesh of the gods and revered throughout the land; when it shone, gold symbolized the Sun god Ra and was important in the afterlife as a symbol of immortality. In the New Kingdom the royal burial chamber was known as the 'House of Gold'.

PALM BRANCH

This symbolized the passing of time, a calendar, as a new branch appeared each month. A notch would be put in the branch to mark the passing of each year in the pharaoh's life. Palm branches also symbolized long life to ancient Egyptians.

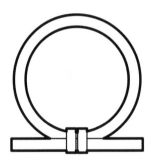

SHEN

The symbol of eternity, this hieroglyphic representation of a rope loop, with no beginning or end, was recognized as a sign of protection. Deities in bird form are often depicted holding the shen. The word comes from *shenu*, which means 'to encircle', and in an elongated form became the cartouche that surrounded the name of pharaohs and other important figures, indicating that the person was under divine protection.

SCARAB

The scarab, or dung beetle, symbolized new life and resurrection. Its action of rolling a ball of dung across the earth represented the journey of the Sun through the sky. In ancient Egyptian paintings it is depicted carrying a huge solar ball. The beetles climbing from the mud represented life coming from the primordial soup and symbolized the creation of life itself.

Scarabs painted with falcon wings symbolize transcendence and protection. The scarab was a popular protective amulet in Egypt.

Mesopotamian Empires

Sometimes referred to as the 'cradle of civilization', Mesopotamia (sited in present-day Iraq), was the birthplace of the first literate societies in the 4th millennium BCE. Three distinct empires flourished – Sumeria, Assyria and Babylon.

SUMERIA

Early Sumerian cities began as small groups of dwelling places centred around a shrine. Eventually, a temple platform, known as a ziggurat, was built to symbolize the connection between Heaven and Earth.

Each shrine was named after a single god, which became part of a single family of gods known as the Anunaki: *Anu* means 'Heaven' while *Na* and *ki* mean 'Earth'. *Anu* was not the god of the Heavens, but was Heaven itself.

ASSYRIA

The main god of Assyria was Ashur, a war god. He was portrayed as a winged disc enclosing a stretched bow ready to let an arrow fly. His consort was Ishtar, queen of the Heavens and goddess of love and war.

BABYLON

Babylon flourished under Hammurabi (1792–1750 BCE). Babylonian mathematicians developed a system of numbering which gave rise to our 60-minute hour and 360° circle. Babylon was a centre of learning and creativity and its Hanging Gardens were one of the seven wonders of the world.

The imposing stepped temple, the ziggurat, was the stairway to Heaven.

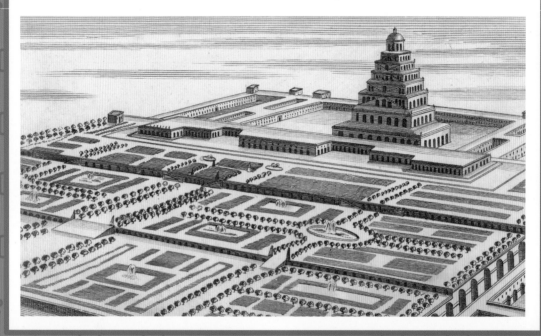

TREE OF LIFE

The Assyrian Tree of Life is one of the most sacred tree symbols. It was a stylized, ornamental expression of a tree that did not exist in physical form but represented the cosmic connection between water, earth and sky. It symbolized the quest to reach from Earth to the Heavens, to achieve contact with the solar power of the Sun. Sometimes it combined the pine and the lotus, symbols of immortality and fecundity.

ZIGGURAT

Derived from the Babylonian word meaning 'to build on a raised area', ziggurats were towers built as terraced pyramids of receding tiers surmounted by a temple. They first appeared in the late 3rd millennium BCE. Sun-baked bricks made up the core of the pyramid with the outer surface covered in fired bricks, many of which were glazed with different colours and astrological symbols. The ziggurats were not used for public ceremonies, but were regarded as the dwelling places of the gods so that the gods could be close to the people. Only priests were allowed to enter the ziggurats and so they assumed very high status in society.

The ziggurat symbolizes the first mound from which the universe was believed to be created and stands as a bridge between Heaven and Earth, that allowed the gods to descend to Earth and man to ascend into Heaven. The Sumerian temples were seen as a cosmic axis, a vertical bond between Heaven and Earth and the Earth and the Underworld, as well as a horizontal bond between lands.

Some ziggurats were built on seven levels, symbolizing seven heavens, seven planets and seven metals associated with them and their respective colours.

According to Sumerian tradition, the bottom level was associated with Saturn and painted black, the second level symbolized Jupiter and was white, the third represented Mercury and was red, the fourth level represented Venus and was blue. The fifth level represented the Earth and was also blue. The sixth level symbolized Mars and was yellow, the final seventh level was grey or silver to symbolize the Moon.

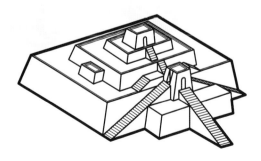

ISHTAR

The Assyrian Moon goddess Ishtar (called Inanna in Sumerian and Astarte in northwest Semitic), was the most important goddess in ancient Mesopotamia. She was also known as the Lady of Vision, the Prophetess and 'She Who Directs Oracles'. Ishtar symbolized the primal force of nature that can create or destroy life.

There are many symbols for Ishtar. She is sometimes depicted wearing a horned crown with a cone in the middle representing the cosmic mountain and an eight-pointed star denoting the planet Venus. She wears a rainbow necklace, the seven colours equating to the seven gates of the Underworld through which she passed, while her girdle depicts the constellations of the zodiac, known to the ancient Mesopotamians as the Houses of the Moon. The 'girdle of Ishtar' represented the Moon calendar of ancient Mesopotamia. In her aspect as goddess of death she is portrayed with serpents, dragons or scorpions. Her warlike manner is revealed as she rides on a lion and carries a mace, a double-headed axe, a spear or a bow. Her Moon connection is symbolized in the crescent she wears on her head and the all-seeing eye of the serpent.

EAGLE-HEADED GOD

The double-headed eagle was a solar symbol which represented the absolute power of royalty and gods of the sky. It symbolizes the spirit of the Sun and the duel between the spiritual world and the lower world. The majestic eagle connects the Heavens and Earth with its swift flight and powerful vision. It is sometimes depicted guarding the Tree of Life, symbol of vegetation and fertility, and shows the symbolic importance of protecting and nurturing both the natural world and kingship to ensure prosperity for Assyria. It represents the spirit of the Sun and the duel between the spiritual world and the lower world.

WINGED SPHINX

The winged sphinx or *lamassu* is an Assyrian word to describe a creature with the body of a winged bull or winged lion, and a bearded human head symbolizing masculine power and sovereignty. Large stone sphinxes were placed at gateways and entrances to palaces in late Assyrian times in order to ward off evil and malign forces. The animal body denoted strength, the wings speed and freedom, while the human head symbolized intelligence. The head also represented the power of the king to protect his people and his ferocity in dealing with enemies.

MARDUK

Marduk, god of the Sun, was the most supreme god of Akkad and its most important city Babylon. He created the Heavens by killing the giant winged dragon Tiamat. Her upper body became the dome of Heaven, the lower part became the Earth and her blood became the oceans. Marduk mixed his own blood with earth and created the first human beings. The other gods regarded him as the chief deity and built him a vast sanctuary, Esaglia in Bablylon. Later he was declared chief god of the whole of Mesopotamia.

BULL DEITIES

The strength and virility of bulls made them a potent symbol throughout the world; in Babylonia, Enlil (Enki) was a central bull deity, 'the savage bull of sky and earth'. Small bronze figures of a bull, representing the god El, were often used to top staffs and rods; serving as portable standards, they represented the power of creation and veneration of the god.

Carved representations of winged bulls were found on important civic buildings in Assyrian cities and represented power, protection and authority. The bull and the lion symbolized potency, masculinity and virility, though they were

also associated with the Moon goddess Ishtar and so carry some ambiguity. Marduk, god of the Sun, is associated with Gudibir, the 'bull of light'. Winged bulls were seen as guardian spirits.

Greece and Rome

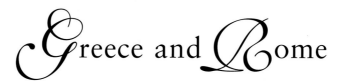

The civilizations of ancient Greece and Rome are considered to have formed the foundation of the modern Western world and their art, literature, politics, law, technology and language were immensely influential. The symbols that were important to each of these two civilizations are closely linked and were taken to many corners of Europe by the empire-forging Romans.

ANCIENT GREECE

Ancient Greek mythology is highly symbolic and relates to the spiritual journey in the material and physical world. The religion was polytheistic, each god or goddess having specific powers and attributes.

A central part of Greek religion were the Mysteries of Eleusis, which were secret annual rituals whose purpose was to worship the gods and thus ensure the continuity of life. The Eleusis initiation rites symbolized the death and rebirth cycle, though no one knows what happened during these mysterious rites.

Mount Olympus, the highest peak in Athens, was the home of the gods. The Olympic games were a way of honouring the gods, and runners carried torches which were also used by the winners to light fires on altars dedicated to Zeus or Athene.

ANCIENT ROME

The Roman Empire was heavily influenced by the Greeks through the Etruscans, who lived in northeast Italy in 900–500 BCE. Most of their gods were shared with the Greeks though their names were changed; Roman gods were invoked to bring good fortune and avert evil.

A she-wolf suckling abandoned twins Romulus and Remus is one of the symbols of ancient Rome. The twins, whose father was Mars, symbolize triumph over adversity since they were thrown into the River Tigris and left for dead. Nike, the winged goddess, was the symbol of military success and is frequently depicted with the laurel wreath, symbol of victory, and a staff with an eagle on top.

Symbols of the gods were found everywhere: the trident of Neptune; the caduceus of Asklepios and later Hermes, which symbolizes protection; the cornucopia, a symbol of plenty and the goddess Copia. Jupiter, the Romans' most significant god, was symbolized by the thunderbolt and the eagle, which is why the eagle features so widely in Roman art and architecture. Today, the thunderbolt or lightning strike lives on, and is used to symbolize danger from electricity pylons.

A view of the summit of Mount Olympus in Athens, mythological home to the Greek gods.

CADUCEUS

The caduceus is depicted as a rod with two serpents entwined. The word *caduceus* originated from 'herald's staff' and was the staff of the god Hermes (Mercury), messenger of the gods. It symbolized protection for the messengers as they carried news of political or commercial matters. It was also associated with Asklepios, the god of healing, and the symbol is still associated with medicine and pharmacy today.

The caduceus is a potent symbol because it included the phallic power of the rod and the Tree of Life, which signifies communication between Heaven and Earth. The two serpents represent duality and the integration of opposites. Also, the fact that snakes could shed their skin symbolized the renewal of life. The caduceus was used by the astrologer priests in the rituals of the Eleusian Mysteries.

OMPHALOS

The omphalos or navel-stone is a symbol of the world. In many traditions the creation of the physical and spiritual universe originates from a navel. An omphalos was placed at Delphi, centre of the worship of the Sun god Apollo, to symbolize its place as the centre of the created universe. It was also a symbol of a channel of communication between the three worlds: the world of the dead in the Underworld, the world of living humans and that of the gods.

LAUREL WREATH

The laurel wreath represents a crowning glory which was bestowed on those who were worthy of honours, including poets, which gives the origin of 'poet laureate'. Military victors in Rome were crowned with laurel wreaths. The laurel is sacred to Apollo, Dionysos, Juno and Daphne.

SERPENT

The serpent is associated with wisdom, power and healing. Cecrops, the legendary founder of Athens, is said to have emerged from the soil as half man, half serpent, and the god of healing, *Aescepulus* in Greek and *Askepulus* in Roman legend, appeared as a snake.

OWL

The owl was the symbol of wisdom and the emblem of Athene, goddess of wisdom and warfare. It is a lunar symbol and is linked to seers with the gift of second sight.

EAGLE

The eagle, whose Latin name is *aquila*, was used as the standard of a Roman legion, and became the emblem of imperial power. The two most important symbols of power and authority in ancient Rome were the staff with an eagle on top and the laurel wreath. The symbols for Zeus (Jupiter in Roman mythology) were a thunderbolt and an eagle. He is depicted wearing a laurel wreath and holding a sceptre.

DOG

In Greek mythology, the three-headed dog
Cerberus guarded the gates of Hades, which
was the name of both a god and the
Underworld. Hades as an Underworld was
divided into several realms: the Elysian Fields
corresponds to Christian Heaven while
Tartarus is similar to Hell, where souls were
tortured for their sins. The god Hades (Pluto
in Roman mythology) is often shown with
snakes which symbolize his infernal origin.

DOVE

The emblem of Athene, goddess of wisdom,
the dove is traditionally the symbol of love.
It is associated with Zeus who was said to
have been fed by doves. The dove is sacred
to Venus, goddess of love.

CUPID

There is some uncertainty about Cupid's
parentage, although the Romans believed him
to be the son of Venus. He is a god of love and
has two kinds of arrows, golden to bring love
and lead to drive the loved one away. He is
sometimes shown with a torch, symbolizing
torch-lit wedding processions, and sometimes
depicted blindfolded, indicating that love is
blind or tying a knot, which represents the
union of the chosen couple.

SCALES OF JUSTICE

Scales of justice are associated with balance, judgement and the weighing of actions. The ancient Greek goddess Themis, goddess of justice, who ruled the world in accordance with universal law, held scales to determine justice which included law, moderation and balance.

VICTORY

The winged goddess Nike (Victory) was an aspect of Athene and is often depicted with a globe and the laurel wreath of the victor. In order to ensure success in battle or competition, sacrifice was made to her before the event and after it was completed.

BEE

In Greek mythology Zeus was raised on milk and honey; the bee was associated with the goddess Artemis and the fertility goddess Demeter, whose priestesses at Eleusis were known as 'bees'. The symbol of a soul, the bee signified the ability to enter the Underworld as Demeter did, and return from it. The honey of bees represented honeyed words of eloquent philosophers such as Plato and Sophocles. Plato asserted that the souls of good and moral men were reincarnated as bees.

PEARL

A symbol of the Moon and linked to women and water, pearls are sacred to the goddess Aphrodite Marina, also called the 'Pearl of the Sea'. Aphrodite's 'Pearly Gate' was a euphemism for her vagina. Pearls were used in funerary rites to assure the dead that they would be reborn, and bags of pearls have been found in coffins in countries as far-flung as Egypt, Vietnam and Mexico.

HARPY

The harpy is a fabulous creature with the head and breasts of a woman and the claws of a vulture and symbolizes the destructive aspect of the feminine principle. It is associated with storms, typhoons and whirlwinds, as well as sudden death. The name means 'snatcher' as harpies supplied the Underworld with souls of people who died before their natural time.

MEDUSA

Medusa was one of the three Gorgons, evil sisters who had hissing serpents for hair, the tusks of boars instead of teeth and hands of brass and golden wings. She was transformed from a beautiful woman after she made love in a temple devoted to Athene, who punished her viciously. Whoever looked at Medusa's face would be instantly turned to stone. She symbolizes fear, in particular men's fear of women's mood changes.

TRISKELION

The triskelion is a three-legged symbol of powerful energy, similar to a swastika but minus one leg. The rotating legs represent physical prowess and in some traditions it is connected to solar and lunar energy.

CORNUCOPIA

The horn of plenty, as the cornucopia is sometimes called, symbolizes inexhaustible bounty. It is filled with fruit and flowers, and its hollow, phallic shapes relates to the union of male and female and is associated with fertility. It represents generosity, fruitfulness and the harvest of the earth.

COMEDY AND TRAGEDY

The mask of comedy used in theatrical performances represents ordinary people in ordinary situations; it may poke fun at human behaviours and human problems.

Masks of tragedy symbolize misfortune as well as the 'tragic flaw' that brings grief and pain to the protagonist. The word tragedy derives from the Greek *tragos*', meaning 'goat', and *oide*, meaning song.

The Celts

The Celts were an Indo-European people who lived in large parts of Central Europe, the Iberian peninsula, Ireland and Britain in pre-Roman times, and spoke several different languages. They developed a system of beliefs and practices which flourished between the 5th and 1st centuries BCE until it was largely destroyed by the Romans.

The Gauls, early Celts in France, developed a system of education based on an oral tradition using Druid priests who officiated at rites including sacrifice. Bards and seers or *filid* preserved their teaching and rituals from generation to generation. The Druids practised divination and predicting the future. The seers observed the patterns made by birds in flight or cracked open the bones of animals to foresee future events and held magical ceremonies to take them to other worlds.

ANIMALS AS SPIRIT GUARDIANS

The Celts worshipped outside in holy groves which had a spirit guardian in the form of an animal. They believed that the gods could take on the shape of animals and that certain animals and people could change form, from a hare, for example, to a man. Many creatures were believed to have magical powers or supernatural wisdom – the cockerel, goose and hare were revered for their sacred associations and were never eaten. Boudicca, warrior queen of the Iceni people, released a hare as an offering to the goddess Andraste so she might succeed in battle, and was rewarded with a great victory.

HEAD SYMBOLS

Heads were an important symbol to the Celts. The heads of their enemies were offered to the gods after battles. Images of heads were found on coins, doorposts, cauldrons and altars because the Celts believed the essence of being, both spiritually and physically, rested in the heads. Carved heads acted as talismans, warding off evil. The head also symbolized divinity and was a sign that life continued after death. Three was a sacred number to the Celts and three-in-one heads were carved, one looking to the past, the next to the present and the third to the future, symbolizing the Celtic view that they could access all three worlds.

THE AFTERLIFE

Central to the Celtic religion and world view was a belief in the afterlife. Druids used herbs in religious practices to aid their entry into other worlds. Celts practised ritual gathering of herbs to ensure their potency and would wear the herb as an amulet. They believed the power came from the Otherworld, a place of darkness and knowledge.

The figure of Cernunnos symbolizes the relationship between the Celts and the natural world.

CELTIC CROSS

The Celtic cross combines the feminine symbol, the circle, and the male cross to form an image that represents union and is linked to fertility. This pre-Christian cross symbolized the four seasons, and the four directions placed over the circle is the symbol of the Earth. Later the Celtic cross was adapted by Christians to represent the connection between Heaven and Earth. Crosses are usually carved with intricate patterns of vine, ivy and other plants which are intertwined and start from a chalice or cup. These symbolize the magical properties of plants and the afterlife.

The Celts had different gods according to where they lived. In Ireland the *Tuatha de Danann* (Tribe of the Goddess Danu) was the name of a group of gods descended from Danu, and can still be seen in the name of the River Danube. The pagan Druids had a practice in which they cut down an oak tree half way up its trunk and placed the upper part across the lower, making a T-shape. This was the Druid symbol for their god Hu, who was also represented as an ox.

SPIRALS

In Celtic symbolism spirals symbolized the Sun and the equinoxes. Single spirals symbolized growth, expanding energy as well as cosmic expansion, and were often paired with snakes and crescent shapes. Spirals were related to the idea of birth and death, the central core was obtained by travelling to the sacred centre and turning back to enter the outer world once more.

An anti-clockwise spiral with widely spaced lines symbolized the full summer Sun. A clockwise, tight spiral represented the winter Sun in its reducing size and strength.

The spiral occuli, double twists which resemble eyes, carved on the entrance stones of sites of religious significance such as Newgrange in Ireland, were associated with the equinoxes.

LOZENGE

The lozenge is usually viewed as a female symbol representing the vulva and the womb of creation, belonging to the Great Mother, who gave birth to us and from whose womb those as yet unborn still rest.

KEY PATTERNS

Key patterns are, in effect, straightened spirals. The interwoven, connected strands lead through a maze-like structure to a centre, the equivalent of the *omphalos* or navel, that sacred point which symbolizes the place of union between Heaven and Earth.

CHEVRON

The chevron is an ancient symbol representing arrows and was found on clothes of chiefs from 3000 BCE. It symbolized high rank and is still used as military insignia today.

CELTIC KNOTS

Celtic knot-work varies from a single design to highly complex patterns. The intricate Celtic knots symbolize the universe and eternity, since they are formed in an unbroken line. In Irish illuminated manuscripts knot illustrations symbolize the perpetual motion of the universe and the entwined cosmic and human interrelationship. Further examples are to be found in the Ardagh chalice and the Tara brooch.

GREEN MAN

The Celtic Green Man, also known as Jack of the Green and Robin of the Woods, was an important fertility god and is associated with the pagan belief that gods and spirits lived in trees. He is a god of vegetation and represents the power of the plant world to bring growth, renewal and energy. He is often shown completely covered in leaves and branches. Carvings of the Green Man were used to protect people and homes. He represents humanity's relationship with trees and woods, the life force and the cycle of renewal and rebirth. Sometimes leaves pour from his mouth, ears and eyes symbolizing the unceasing growth and abundance of nature.

Carvings of the Green Man, in stone and wood, were used as a protection against evil. He appears throughout Britain and Europe especially in connection with spring fertility festivals and has been found in carvings on the Indian sub-continent.

CERNUNNOS

Cernunnos, the 'Horned Sacred One', was the god of all animals and the lord of the natural world for the Celts. The half-man and half-beast symbolizes the closely bound relationship between the Celts and the natural world. The antlers that grow on his head represent the eternal cycle of regeneration, and where he is shown with a snake in his hand, it doubles the identification with renewal since the snake sheds its skin and is renewed. He is a male hunter-god and is associated with animals and fertility. The torc and necklaces he wears denote power and status.

CAULDRON

To the Celts water was the essence of life and a magical fluid that brought truth and power. The cauldron or cup was the container for water and became imbued with a spiritual power of its own. It symbolizes rebirth and plenty. The Irish god Dagda, whose name means 'the all-powerful god', had a cauldron that provided a never-ending supply of food.

The Celtic ritual cauldron discovered in Gundestrup, Denmark is decorated with sacred figures and symbols. According to the *Mabinogi of Branwen*, there was a cauldron of rebirth within which the dead were placed and were reborn the next day; however, other cauldrons had sacrificial uses. One was filled with wine or beer and the old king was drowned on the last day of the feast of Samhain.

SHEELA-NA-GIG

The figure of an unattractive naked female displaying grotesquely large genitals is found in Celtic and medieval stonework, particularly in Ireland (this depiction is based on a famous carving at Kilpeck in the UK). The origins of the figure's name, which has many spelling variants, are uncertain and there are conflicting theories about its significance. Some believe the figure was carved above doorways and windows to ward off evil, others that it is a warning against female lust, seen as sinful and hideous in medieval times. The most popular theory, however, is that it represents a Celtic or pagan fertility or mother goddess. Its resemblance to the Viking creator goddess, Ormguddinu, would support this theory.

Scandinavia

The early Scandinavians worshipped many gods. The Norse warrior Vikings worshipped Odin or Wotan as the god of memory and thought. Thor, the god of thunder and lightning, symbolized both power and protection. Freya was a warrior goddess and the goddess of love, though she was also venerated for her beauty. Her brother Freyr was the horned god of fertility, of power and success in battle.

LONGBOATS

As a warring tribe, the Vikings put great store in their longboats, which were designed to strike fear into their enemies. They were the symbol of speed, power and supremacy. These vessels also represented the journey taken to the afterlife as ships were used in burials, ensuring the safe passage to the next life. Hel was the Norse goddess of the Underworld where the dead lived, and the place became known as Hel.

LUCKY TREES

In Scandinavia it was customary to have a guardian or lucky tree planted next to your house. Symbolic offerings were then made to it and beer or some other liquid poured over its roots. In Norway, the World Tree was the giver of nourishment and a source of healing.

RUNIC ALPHABET

Before it was replaced by a Latin alphabet during Christianization, the Scandinavian people used a runic alphabet. The runic alphabet does not use horizontal strokes, a peculiarity attributed to the fact that runes were usually carved on the edge of pieces of wood and horizontal lines would have been lost in the grain of the wood. Even after Christianization, runes continued to be used for specialized purposes in Scandinavia, up until the early 20th century.

Runes are considered to have a magical association. The earliest runic inscriptions were not used as a writing system and it has been considered that they were magical signs, used as charms or for divination. The name 'rune' itself is thought to mean 'secret, something hidden' and suggests that knowledge of the runes was possibly esoteric, or restricted to an elite.

*Viking longboats were used in burial rituals and
were symbolic of the journey to the afterlife.*

F U TH A R K H N I A

S T B M L R

RUNES

Runes were used to write Germanic
languages before and shortly after the
Christianization of the British Isles and
Scandinavia, and the word comes from *runa*,
which meant 'secret or something hidden'.
However, in the Finnish tradition there is a
legend that the Norse god Odin invented the
runic alphabet, but a mortal named Kettil
Runske stole three rune staffs from Odin and
learned their runes and magic, and so
brought the mystical knowledge of the gods
to Earth for human use. Early runes were not
a simple writing system, but sacred magical
signs used as charms and for divination.

The original 16 symbols of the alphabet
were changed and added to over the years in
different countries, but whatever the number,
they contained ideas, words, fertility symbols
and concepts and were inscribed on wood or
stone. Each rune represents a word rather
than a letter and specific runes were
associated with the Sun and the Moon, and
funerary runes were linked to death. They
were believed to have supernatural powers to
avert danger, and 'the drawing of lots' and
then reading the runes that fell was a form of
divination, a way of seeing the future. Runes
were included in magic and religious rituals
and were used to write magical incantations.

ANSUZ

The equivalent of the letter A, this rune
represented messages and signals and was
associated with the mouth as the source of
divine speech. Ansuz was linked with rivers
and the trickster god Loki.

THE RUNIC SWASTIKA

Pagan tombstones in Scandinavia were found to have carved runic swastikas. The closed 'arms' symbolized the return of the dead to the womb of Mother Earth. The idea of returning to the earth after death and the recycling of the dead was common in the beliefs of pagans. The runic swastika was also known as Thor's hammer, which he used to drive off giants who threatened the Scandinavian people. Adolf Hitler adopted the runic double *sigrune*, the victory rune associated with the Sun, as a symbol of the Nazi Third Reich.

BOAR

The ferocity of wild boar made them a natural symbol of war, protection from hurt or defeat and kingship. There is evidence of a Scandinavian custom of a Yule boar, which has connections to cereal crops, and it is thought that there may have been an ancient custom of boar sacrifice. Boars were also linked to magic and the Underworld.

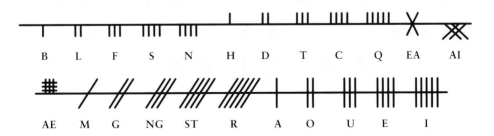

OGHAM ALPHABET

Distantly related to the runic alphabet, the Ogham Tree alphabet has 25 symbols made up of a series of horizontal and vertical lines. Of these, 23 (above) are named after trees (the other two mean 'grove' and 'sea'). This alphabet was used primarily for divination and augury by seers and Druids, rather than as a form of traditional written communication. Nearly all the Ogham inscriptions that exist are on burial stones, landmarks or stones that indicate property boundaries. Ogham symbols were believed to be under the control of the Celtic god of speech, Ogma.

Aztec Empire

The Aztecs flourished from around 1325 CE until their demise during the 16th century at the hands of the conquistadors and the diseases that the Spanish brought to the New World. The Aztecs founded their chief city, Tenochtitlan, on the site of present-day Mexico City. They worshipped hundreds of deities, each of whom ruled over aspects of nature such as the weather and over the actions of humans, and built ceremonial centres where religious rites, including human sacrifice, took place.

AZTEC GODS

Huitzilopochtli was the war/Sun god whose temple on the Great Pyramid in Tenochtitlan was consecrated with the sacrifice of thousands of lives. Huitzilopochtli was also called the 'Blue Heron Bird' or the 'Eagle' and was said to live in the Seventh Heaven of Aztec mythology, which is represented as blue. He symbolized the Sun and was believed to struggle to keep the Sun from being overcome by the forces of the night. Each dawn represents his success, a daily victory against the darkness.

Another important god was the hermaphrodite Ometecuhtli, 'Two-Lord', who reigned over the other gods – the red god of fire, the yellow Sun god and the white evening star god. The oldest god was Hueueteotl, the 'old, old deity' whose sacred place was the fireplace in every home. This cult of fire meant that the chief duty of the temple priests was to maintain the sacred fire.

SACRED MAIZE

Maize was so important to the Aztecs that they thought of themselves as being formed from it. They called maize dough *toneuhcayotl*, 'our flesh', and in some creation myths the first people were made from soft maize dough. The people worshipped numerous corn gods to ensure good harvests of the vital crop. Images of corn are found in carvings on altars. The majority of the great cultures in the region believed that maize was the flesh of the gods, which may have been the origin of the widespread practice of human sacrifice. They returned the favour of the gods by giving them human flesh.

CARVINGS

The symbols depicted in this chapter were generally embedded in intricate carvings and would seldom have stood alone. The calendar glyphs, however, were individual and formed complete symbols in themselves.

The Aztec Sun Stone.

AZTEC CALENDAR OR SUN STONE

This famous symbol of Mexico, carved in stone during the 15th century CE, was dedicated to the Aztec sacrificial Sun god, Tonatiuh. The 3.6 metre (12 ft) Aztec Calendar or Sun Stone has the face of the Sun god at its centre with rings encircling the face to symbolize different periods, and days and events in the natural world. The whole known universe is represented in the Sun Stone.

Aztec calendars used symbols and numbers to record and measure time.

There were two different types of calendar: the civil calendar, linked to the seasons, had 365 days divided into 18 periods or months containing 20 days each. This left five days over that served as a transition between the old and new year and were used for festivities. The religious calendar had 260 days, with 20 periods each containing 13 days with a different symbol dedicated to a specific god. The gods were regarded as good or bad, so each day would be influenced by the temperament of that particular deity and suggest the mood for the day.

TRIPLE DEATH MASK

This represents the vital cycle of life. The Aztecs believed everyone has three distinct phases: youth, old age and death. Masks were worn during religious and divinatory ceremonies and were used in grave offerings.

EARTH

Mother Earth – Pachamama – is sacred to Mesoamericans and all forms of offerings are made to her as petitions, as thanksgiving or to bring good luck. She is a fertility goddess with links to planting and harvesting.

WATER

Water symbolized the chaos out of which the world arose and the source of life. The Aztecs called human blood *chalchiuatl* or 'precious water'.

CORN

The earliest form of maize was a wild cereal grass called *teosinte*, which was gathered and eaten *c.*7000–5000 BCE. Maize became a staple food to the hunter-gatherers of Mesoamerica and though its preparation was time-consuming, the dough made from corn was used to make flat bread, maize water provided the first drink of the day and maize was the main ingredient of the soup *atolli*.

The Aztecs worshipped a number of corn gods. Xilonen, the goddess of young maize cobs, is depicted as a virginal girl.

HEART

The heart symbolized the centre of man, religion and love, the unifying life-principle. Both Maya and Aztec killed human sacrifices by taking out their hearts, believing that their gods desired this. The beating heart represented the body's Sun that activated every aspect of human life, and so thousands of people were sacrificed to the Sun every year to ensure its continued power. The heart sacrifice meant releasing the life-blood to bring about regeneration.

JAGUAR

The jaguar is one of the most potent symbols in the Americas. It represents power, psychic knowledge, sorcery, kingship, the earth and fertility, and is the symbol of royalty and bravery. A nocturnal animal, it is linked with the Moon and the secrets of the dark spirit world. It represented the animal nature of Tezcatlipoca, the Aztec god of night and dark deeds. The Aztecs believed that when the Sun journeyed in the Underworld at night, he took the form of a jaguar.

As a symbol the jaguar was honoured, but it was also feared because of its predatory nature and destructive aspect. Shamans wore jaguar skins or jaguar masks which symbolized their ability to protect or to destroy as well as to travel in the spirit world.

EARTHQUAKE/HEARTBEAT

In the Nahuatl language of the Aztecs, Olin means movement, as in heartbeat or earthquake. The Olin symbolizes the centre of the world or the heartbeat that keeps the world in existence. Four Olin appear at the centre of the Sun Stone, representing the Earthquake epoch.

An artefact known as the Olin Bowl survives from the Aztec civilization. In its centre is an olin design and the bowl is believed to have received the still-beating hearts of victims of sacrifice, offered to the earth god to prevent earthquakes and destruction.

DEATH EYE

The Aztecs believed that death was not to be feared and that to die in battle or in a sacrificial rite was an honour. The death eye, symbolized by a circle with a straight line bisecting it, is found on pictures of the gods, including the gods of death and wind.

COYOTE

The coyote symbolizes the ancient shape-shifting god, Huehuecoyotl, or 'Old Man Coyote'. It is associated with sexuality, strength and cunning.

SKULLS

Skulls in Aztec art represent the sacrificed victims whose deaths ensured the prevention of earthquakes and the continuation of the world. Gods of death are routinely depicted with exposed skull heads and, often, with the spine partially shown, symbolizing the continuity of life and death which can never be truly separated.

The god of death Mictlantechtli is frequently shown wearing a skull with large teeth. Other deities were described with skulls for heads and decorated with bones. This skeletal imagery reflects the Aztec view of death as part of life, and that through death and sacrifice abundance and health can be assured. A skull decorated with shell and jade would be buried in the tomb of an Aztec noble who showed no fear in going into the next world.

FEATHERED SERPENT

A serpent covered in bright green feathers of the quetzal bird was the emblem of Quetzalcoatl, the god of sky and Earth. The dual nature of the serpent, protective-destructive, figures in myths which indicate that the destructive aspect must be mastered so that the constructive, ordered aspect may then emerge.

The double-headed serpent symbolized life-giving rain and was associated with the rites of Thaloc, god of mountains, rain and springs. The Aztec double-headed rattlesnake is found in carvings which relate to the Earth goddess Coatlicue.

CAPTURED CITY

The conquest of others was vitally important to the Aztecs, for in capturing a city they obtained the source of sacrificial victims to appease their gods. The symbol of the captured city is a person being held by his forelock with the design of the specific city being inscribed above the defeated person's head.

Maya Civilization

The Maya civilization of Central America, which emerged about 250 CE, produced a wealth of symbolism – even their cities were symbolic, ceremonial sites whose walls were carved with sacred symbols. Their woven textiles were abundantly decorated with symbolic designs which the Maya understood; a common motif was a diamond shape representing the universe and the path the Sun takes as it moves through the Heavens.

MATHEMATICS

The Maya mathematical system was the most sophisticated ever developed in the Americas. It involved the use of symbols – a dot represented one unit, a straight line represented five units, a shell represented zero. Their numbering system was based on units of 20 rather than our current 10. At the time most of the world's civilizations had no concept of zero, yet the Maya knew of its crucial importance. The Maya set of mathematical symbols allowed even uneducated people to add and subtract for trade and commerce.

Mathematics was central to the Maya world. In wall paintings mathematicians and scribes can be seen with number scrolls hanging from their arms. The first mathematician identified on a glyph was a female figure. Different numbers are depicted as different goddesses and gods.

Some numbers were considered more sacred than others. The number 20 was special since it represented the number of fingers and toes a human being could count on. Five represented the number of digits on a hand or foot. The number 13 was sacred, as 13 Maya gods ruled 13 Heavens, and 400 was sacred because it represented the number of Maya gods of the night.

Highly decorative carved panels depict numerous Maya gods.

CALENDAR

The Maya calendar was based on the movement of the Earth and Sun, which indicated a knowledge of astronomy unrivalled by any other culture of their day. The ancient Maya used 17 different calendars based on their knowledge of the cosmos. Calculated by priests, the two most important calendars are the 'Haab' based on the Earth's rotation round the Sun and the sacred calendar, 'Tzolk'in', based on the rotation of the Pleiades constellation. The Maya used the visestimal system of counting based on the number 20.

The most significant and oldest calendar had a 260-day cycle and was found throughout Mesoamerica and is still used in certain regions, such as the Guatemalan highlands. Known as the Tzolk'in, it was combined with another 365-day calendar called the Haab (shown above, with the Maya God of Time at the centre) to make a synchronized cycle which lasted 52 Haabs. This was called the Calendar Round. Contained within the Tzolkin and Haab calendars were smaller cycles; one of 13 days, the trecena, and 20 days, the veintena, respectively.

Another type of calendar, known as the Long Count, was used to record longer periods of time and to note calendar dates – that is, events which happened in relation to other dates. It is based on the number of days since a mythical starting point and could be extended to any future point. The Long Count calendar was based on a positional notation system. Each position represented a multiple of the number of days. The Maya numeral system had a base of 20 and each unit of a given position represented 20 times the unit of the position that preceded it. There was an exception to this for the second-place value, which represented 18 x 20, or 360 days, which is nearer to the solar year than 20 x 20 which would give 400 days. However, the cycles of the Long Count are independent of the solar year. They used glyphs or symbols to represent each day and month. In the language of the Maya script *k'in* means day and Sun and the symbolic *k'in* sign represents a day-blooming flower. The cycles of time were plotted on decorative calendar charts.

THE WORLD TREE

The World Tree or *Wacah Chan* is a powerful Maya symbol of the creation and organization of the world order. Its roots reach to *Xibalba*, the Underworld, and its branches stretch into the Heavens. The World Tree is symbolized by the Milky Way. On 13 August, the date that the Maya believed the world was created, the Milky Way stands erect at dawn, going through the zenith from north to south. It becomes the axis of the Earth–Sky, 'the raised-up sky'. This depiction is taken from The Tablet of the Cross at The Temple of the Cross at Palenque.

VULTURE

To the Maya the vulture, who fed on entrails, symbolized death. However, it also represented regeneration and transformation in the recycling of dead carrion, to sustain life on Earth. In the Mayan calendar the vulture is said to control the vital storms of the dry season and is associated with astrological water signs.

JAGUAR

The Maya Sun god, Ahau Kin, was believed to transform into the Jaguar god when he travelled through the Underworld at night. The jaguar was the symbol of strength and courage in Mesoamerica, and Maya kings wore jaguar skins to signify bravery.

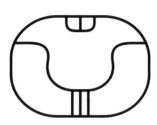

MAIZE

In the Maya creation myth, the gods Huracan and Gucumatz made the first humans from maize. This is celebrated in the Temple of the Foliated Cross in the city of Palenque, where they are depicted either side of a giant cob of maize which is topped by a human head. In one myth, after many attempts to make humans from mud and then wood, the gods finally mixed their own blood with maize flour and were successful. This is depicted in the Maya image of a man sprouting from a stalk of maize.

SERPENT

The Vision Serpent was worshipped by the Maya. They believed that those who achieved a state of spiritual ecstasy could access the ancestors or the deities by following the coils of this great snake. This involved blood-letting ceremonies, in which the chosen one's blood spilled on to ceremonial papers which were then burned. As the smoke curled upwards, the serpent would appear with the ancestor or god emerging from its mouth.

During coronation ceremonies, the king contacted ancestor spirits through the Vision Serpent to ask for their guidance and blessing.

SUN

The Sun was the symbol of royal authority. Kings were often referred to as *K'inich Ahaw*, Sun-eyed Lord. In Maya script *k'in* means both 'Sun' and 'day'.

WATER LILY

For the Maya the water lily symbolized rebirth and regeneration. It featured in frescoes and carvings.

Inca Empire

According to Inca history, the early Incas believed that prior to this world there was a previous civilization which died out because a comet or asteroid wiped out the known world. Depictions of a comet symbol on a rock at the Sillustani burial ground record this event, and next to the comet there is a spiral symbol which, for the Incas, represented the gateway to the next dimension.

INCA GODS

The Inca empire emerged in South America in 1200 CE and lasted until 1533 when the last emperor was killed by Francisco Pizarro. The Inca worshipped a pantheon of gods and goddesses, the most important of whom were Pachamama and Pacha Camac, Earth Mother and Earth Father, and the Sun god, Inti. Other significant gods were: the snake, which represents the intellect; the puma, which represents courage and life lived completely in the present; and the condor, which symbolizes balance and life in the future as well as the possibility of life in another dimension. In order to propitiate the gods, the Inca made offerings, and guinea pigs were a special sacrifice at any important feast. Traces of this ancient religion can be found in the present interpretation of Catholicism in Peru.

In the Catholic cathedral in Cuzco, the painting of the *Last Supper* has at its centre a roasted guinea pig.

SACRED SITES

Everything was sacred to the Inca and they built temples such as Machu Picchu as places of pilgrimage and sanctuary. Their temples were highly decorated with carvings and statues made of gold and silver. The Inca mined gold and silver extensively and believed that gold was 'the sweat of the Sun' and silver was the 'tears of the Moon'. The sacred sites contained 'power spots', rocks where spiritual energy was amplified, and sometimes the Incas carved seats or niches into them so that believers could absorb the energies by sitting on the rock.

SUN FESTIVAL

The Inca believed they were descended from the Sun and the Inti Raymi, or Sun Festival, was the most important festival in their calendar. It was performed every year on 21 June, the winter solstice in the Southern Hemisphere. During the ceremonies and rituals the Inca worshipped the Sun god, Apu Inti, and prayed that the Sun would not abandon them, for if it disappeared they would not be able to grow their crops of maize and potatoes and would starve.

Huayna Picchu towers above the ruins of Machu Picchu, whose temples were places of pilgrimage.

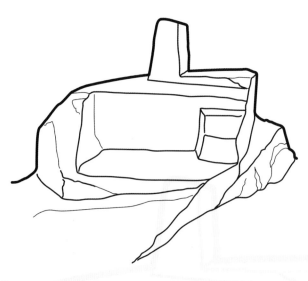

CALENDAR

The Inca used a precise solar calendar to follow the movement of the Sun in order to choose the optimal time for planting and harvesting. Temples were built to allow the light to fall at a particular point or through an opening during the solstice and equinox. The observation of the equinoxes was made using 'shadow clocks' made of stone, such as the *Intihuatana*, 'the hitching-post of the Sun' at Machu Picchu (pictured above), and was central to their Sun cult. At midday on the two equinoxes, the Sun would stand directly above the post, casting no shadow. The Inca believed it was then hitched to the post and held ceremonies to halt the Sun's northward movement in the sky. The *Intihuatana* is probably the final remaining sundial of the Inca: the rest were destroyed by the conquering Spanish, who regarded them as pagan, but they never discovered the location of Machu Picchu, despite suspecting its existence.

The Inca had a calendar based on observation of both the Sun and Moon and their relationship to the stars. They recorded 12 lunar months which were linked to festivals and to the agricultural cycle. The Chibcha tribe calendar had a 30-day month. Every third year was made up of 13 moons, the others having 12. The Inca Veracocha established a calendar of 12 months, each beginning with a New Moon, and his successor Pachacuti, finding some confusions with this, built Sun towers in order to make observations to correct the calendar. This developed into the sidereal-lunar type calendar based on the sidereal month of 27⅓ days. It was made up of 328 nights and began on 8 or 9 June, coinciding with the rising of the Pleiades (an open star cluster in the constellation of Taurus) just after sunset. It ended on the first full Moon after the June solstice, which is the winter solstice in the Southern Hemisphere.

PUMA

The puma symbolizes courage, internal strength and the present. The last is particularly significant as living in the moment was central to the Inca philosophy. The puma was so important to the Inca that some believe they designed their capital city Cuzco in the shape of this powerful animal. Lake Titicaca means 'the meeting place of the pumas' and the Sun temple in Cuzco has puma-teeth designs.

CONDOR

In Inca myth the condor is an avatar, a manifestation of the Sun. The largest bird in the world, it symbolizes power, regeneration and nobility and connects Heaven and Earth. Condor feathers are used by shamans in their purification rituals to clear away bad spirits. The condor represents perfect balance and the future as well as the possibility of living on after death in another dimension.

SNAKE

The snake symbolizes intellect, knowledge and the past. It was regarded as the deity of the Underworld and was part of the trio of deities of central importance to the Inca: the condor was seen as the guardian of the heavens and the puma, guardian of the Earth, the world of humans. The snake is a positive symbol for the Inca, but the conquistadors saw it as a sign that the Inca were worshippers of evil and, although they destroyed many other carvings, did not destroy examples of the snake shown, for instance, on buildings in order to ensure that others would share their negative view of the civilization they destroyed.

RELIGIOUS SYMBOLS: WESTERN AND MIDDLE-EASTERN

Symbols rooted in Western religious traditions abound and many symbols cross religious boundaries. These symbols are drawn from early Judaism and the mystical Kabbalah, through the various permutations of Christianity and on to the more esoteric traditions of Freemasonry, Gnosticism and Rosicrucianism. Islam, too, has contributed a wealth of religious symbols that stand for its beliefs and complex ideas.

There is a great deal of shared symbolism in Western religious traditions. The star, for example, is an important symbol carried from the earliest belief systems. Seen in the dark sky, the brilliance of the star came to represent illumination of the spirit,

vigilance, constancy and guidance. In the Bible, Christ is described as a 'shining morning star' and the Bethlehem star guided the magi to his birthplace. In Islam, the five-pointed star symbolizes ascendancy and it appears with the crescent on many flags. Muslims see the star as a symbol of God that reassures those whose faith is troubled. In Freemasonry, it appears as the Blazing Star, while for Gnostics it is the seven-pointed mystic star. In mystic traditions it is known as the pentagram. Each religious tradition uses the star symbol to reflect its own beliefs, but the constant view is that it brings light to guide the human soul away from darkness into spiritual illumination.

Judaism and the Kabbalah

Judaism has existed for over 4,000 years and Israel, as the Jewish spiritual home, is a symbol of the Promised Land given to them by God. The First Temple was erected in Jerusalem, with King David's son Solomon as a symbol of man's connection with God. It was finally destroyed in 70 CE; the Wailing Wall is all that remains and is a sacred place of pilgrimage for Jews, symbolizing their separation from the First Temple.

Judaism is a monotheistic religion whose laws came from the covenant or agreement that God made with Abraham, that the Jews would be God's chosen ones if they followed the laws given to Moses, which were recorded in the Torah. The study of the Torah is central to the Jewish faith and it is one of its most sacred symbols, representing the spiritual world and all the laws that govern Judaism. In the synagogue, the Torah is housed in a special cupboard known as the 'Ark of Covenant', which is attached to a wall that faces the holy city of Jerusalem.

KABBALAH

Kabbalah is the mystical arm of Judaism, which interprets God's essence as ten spheres, *sephiroth*, through which followers must pass in order to know the divine spirit. In the Kabbalist system the ultimate light which takes us to Keter, the top dimension, is too powerful for humans unless they have understood the codes of Kabbalah. They believe that for 99 per cent of our existence we are shielded from this wisdom by our ignorance. The 'curtains' conceal the light so we are not blinded by it. In following the discipline of practice, the initiate can move from Malkhut at the bottom, the darkest dimension that is our physical world, and progress through the *sephiroth* to the point which is closest to 'the Endless World'.

Kabbalists believe that its teachings contain long-hidden keys to the secret of the universe and also to the mysteries of the heart and soul. The doctrines of Kabbalah were kept secret from outsiders by a highly complicated series of esoteric symbols including some numerical ones.

The Wailing Wall, the western wall in the old city of Jerusalem, is a most sacred Jewish site.

STAR OF DAVID

The two interlocking triangles that form
the Star of David symbolize the marriage of
opposites, bonds of flesh and spirit as well as
active and passive principles. The Star of
David is believed to have originated from the
shield of King David, who unified Judah and
Israel, and it is the emblem of Judaism. In
earlier times it was known as the Seal of
Solomon or Solomon's Shield. It is also
known as the Magen David and is the
symbol most commonly associated with
Judaism. From the 17th century the Star
of David was placed on the outside of
synagogues to identify a place of Jewish
worship, in much the same way that
Christians used a cross to indicate a
Christian place of worship.

MENORAH

The traditional seven-branched candelabrum
used in Jewish rituals is one of the oldest
symbols of the Jewish faith. Each branch
represents one of the seven days of creation
and candles were usually lit one at a time
over seven days. It also symbolized the
planets, the days of the week and the seven
levels of Heaven. Occult tradition associated
it with the Hebrew archangels of the seven
celestial spheres.

The original menorah was described in the
Bible as being made of gold with bowls in
the shape of almonds to hold oil. It resembles
the Tree of Life and so is linked to spiritual
regeneration. Its origins probably lie in the
ancient Babylonian World Tree. The name of
the central column is Shamash, which is the
name of the Babylonian Sun god.

TREE OF LIFE

This symbol of everlasting creation has its roots in the Underworld, its trunk in the Earthly world and its branches stretching into the Heavens, symbolizing the unending link between all three. It also symbolizes the ability to contact other worlds.

The Tree of Life appears to be a universal symbol, representing the belief that humans can ascend from their lower nature to achieve spiritual awareness and Heavenly connection. Also known as the Cosmic Tree, it is often depicted with spheres, lights, fruits or stars in its branches, which symbolize the planets of lunar and solar cycles.

The inverted tree is found in Jewish Kabbalah and in the Hindu *Bhagavad Gita*. It symbolizes God in the Heaven as the source of all life which flows through everything and in every direction. It also emphasizes the concept of 'as it is above, so it is below' – the tree can be reversed, but the life force is the same.

MEZZUZAH

The mezzuzah is both a small scroll, called a *klaf* in Hebrew, and the case which covers it. The scroll is usually a handwitten parchment containing two short sections from the Torah, beginning 'Hear, O Israel! The Lord our God, The Lord is One...' The mezzuzah is a reminder of God's presence. The talismanic case symbolizes divine protection and is fixed on the right-hand side of door posts in Jewish homes to invoke divine blessings. Some Jews, when passing through a doorway, touch the mezzuzah with their forefinger, then kiss their finger to express their devotion to the Torah.

UNIVERSAL ALPHABET

Kabbalists believed that the letters of the Hebrew alphabet transcend religion, race and geography and that the letters themselves are instruments of power. The Hebrew word for 'letter' translates as 'pulse or vibration', an energetic manifestation that underpins the whole of our universe since all matter is energy or vibration. This 'Natural Alphabet' as it was also called, could reveal all that was to be known about God and the universe.

Different combinations release different emotions, spiritual awareness and healing, and by meditating on them Kabbalists progress on their path to Keter. The 72 Names of God, for instance, are not names assigned to people, but a series of three-letter sequences that bring positive change and spiritual energy into the initiate's life. Each sequence has a different purpose and is scanned from left to right. According to the Kabbalah, there are 72 powers assigned to God.

ALEPH	BET	GIMMEL	DALED	HAY	VAV
ZAYIN	CHET	YET	YUD	KAF	LAMED
MEM	WUN	SAMECH	AYIN	PAY	TSADEE
KIF	RESH	SHIN	TAF		

TETRAGRAMMATON

Though God's name was revealed to Moses, it was too holy to be spoken and so it was represented symbolically in the Tetragrammaton, the letters Y, H, W, H. The letters were thought to have come from the Hebrew verb 'to be': HVH *Hovah* means 'to be'; HYH *Hayah* means 'was'; and YHYH *Yi-yeh* means 'will be'. It emphasizes God's absolute being and that He is without beginning or end. Vowels were added to give *Yahweh*, which is sometimes translated as Jehovah.

The Tetragrammaton was inscribed on the rod of Aaron and the ring of Solomon – both

symbols of power and authority and each associated with divination. In Kabbalah, the Tetragrammaton symbolizes life and mystical power. It is often written on plaques in synagogues and in the home as a reminder of God's power and continual presence. The Tetragrammation was believed to have healing and magical powers.

SEPHIROTI IIC TREE

This Tree of Life is an arrangement of ten interconnected spheres which represent the central system of the Jewish Kabbalistic tradition. It symbolizes a map of the universe and the psyche, a blueprint of the creation of the cosmos, and lays out the path to spiritual enlightenment.

Kabbalists divided the universe of these ten spheres into four worlds arranged into a 'Sephirothic Tree'. The circles represent the numbers one to ten which are connected by 22 channels, which represent the 22 letters of the Hebrew alphabet. The ten *sephiroth* are divided into four realms: Atziluth, the world of the supernatural, beyond which is nothing 'ain'; Beriah, the creative world of archetypes and ideals; Yetsirah, the world of formation; and Assiah, the material world, manifest creation.

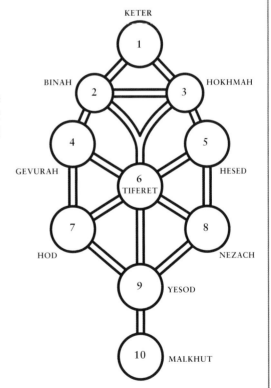

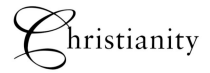Christianity

Since its earliest times, Christianity has found expression in symbolism, through art, church architecture, icons and decoration. Alongside Islam, Christianity is the world's most widespread religion. Some Christians believe that Christ is the ultimate symbol: He represents Heaven and Earth through his divine and human natures; and Fire and Air because of His descent into Hell and his ascension into Heaven, which are symbolized by the tomb and His resurrection.

CHRISTIAN SYMBOLS AS TEACHERS

Christian symbolism is used to teach and present religious truths and because of the visual nature of symbols they make precepts easier to grasp. For example, the halo is a luminous cloud or circle of light which signals the glory of God or the divinity of the Virgin Mary. Anyone familiar with Christian symbols knows that divine grace is attached to the person represented. The aureole surrounds the whole body while, the halo or nimbus surrounds the head.

Similarly, the ichthus, or fish symbol, was used by early Christians to point the way to secret meeting places, as it was easily recognized by adherents to the faith.

THE SYMBOLISM OF THE CROSS

One of the earliest and most enduring Christian symbols is the cross. It has particular resonance for Christians since it is the symbol of Christ's suffering. In truth, however, in earliest Christian executions, the victim was more likely to be crucified on a stake, since there are no references to death on a cross prior to the time of Constantine. Nonetheless, the sign of the cross is recognized as central to Christian faith and is used in the Catholic Mass, Christian blessings and as a sign of belief in the death and resurrection of Christ. The cross is also a symbol of forgiveness and signifies the union of the divine with the human. The vertical represents the divine or Heaven, and the horizontal the human and Earth. Other significant symbols are the fish, the crown of thorns, the lamb and the trinity.

The halo symbolizes a circle of illumination which represents the glory of God.

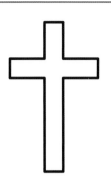

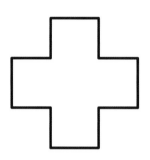

LATIN CROSS

The Latin cross, the *crux immissa*, is the simplest and most common form of cross. A crucifix with Jesus on the cross is more common in Catholic settings, representing the sacrifice of Christ, whereas the empty cross is more widespread in Protestant churches and symbolizes the resurrection.

GREEK CROSS

This is an ancient form and is associated with St Andrew, the Christian disciple who is believed to have introduced Christianity to Russia, and who was crucified on this equal-armed cross. It was popular among persecuted Christians because it could be easily disguised and transformed into a secret sign.

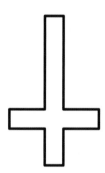

CELTIC CROSS

The Celtic cross was adapted by Christians to represent the connection between Heaven and Earth. It is usually carved with intricate patterns of vine, ivy and other plants which are intertwined and start from a chalice or cup.

INVERTED CROSS

This is known as the cross of St Peter, who asked to be crucified upside down as he did not believe he was worthy enough to be crucified in the same position as Christ. As popes are spiritual descendants of St Peter, it is often used in connection with the papacy and is found on papal thrones and tombs. It also symbolizes humility.

CROSS OF CALVARY

The three steps at the foot of the cross symbolize the Hill of Calvary, and faith, hope and charity. The road to Calvary, via Dolorosa, was where Christ carried the cross on which he was crucified. It is the emblem of Christianity.

TRIUMPHANT CROSS WITH ORB

The cross represents Christianity and the orb represents the Earth and symbolizes Christ's triumph over the world as well as the defeat of Paganism by Christianity. It is often found on Christ's sceptre in Christian art.

ICTHUS

The fish is an early Christian symbol and marked graves in Roman catacombs where persecuted Christians would meet in secret to follow their faith. It is based on the initial Greek letters of Jesus Christ, son of God, *Iesous Christos Theou Yios Soter*, which spelled *Icthus*, the Greek word for 'fish'. Jesus also referred to his disciples as the 'fishers of men' and early Christian fathers called the followers of the faith *pisculi* or fish.

STAR

A star shining in a dark sky symbolizes the spirit struggling for and achieving enlightenment. The Bible calls Jesus the 'Morning Star'. Stars guided the three Magi to Bethlehem for the birth of Jesus and they symbolize divine guidance and knowledge that may come from the Heavens. The Virgin Mary, the Queen of Heaven, is often depicted wearing a crown of stars.

GRAIL

The grail combines two Celtic religious symbols – the cauldron of the Dagda and the chalice of kingship. Later the concept became transformed in Christian symbolism after a goblet was used by Joseph of Arimathea to collect the blood of Christ during his crucifixion. Thereafter, the chalice came to represent the sacred heart and the blood symbolized the bestowal of divine grace.

At the Last Supper a goblet was used to hold wine when Christ told his disciples that the bread and wine were his body and blood, and by drinking from the goblet the disciples would receive his divine grace and take forward the message of Christianity. The chalice used in the Mass at the Eucharist symbolizes this ceremony.

The chalice is a female symbol of the vagina because of its concave shape, while the blade, knife or sword is the symbol of the penis.

AGNUS DEI – LAMB OF GOD

This is a symbol of Christ as the Paschal lamb and also a symbol for Christians who follow 'the Good Shepherd'. The lamb is the symbol of purity, innocence, redemption and renewal. As the sacrificial lamb, it symbolizes the sacrifice of Christ who died in order to redeem the world: 'Lamb of God which taketh away the sins of the world'. The pure, unblemished Paschal lamb was sacrificed by the Jews at Passover as a symbolic ritual to take away the sins of the tribe. The Lamb of God is often depicted with a cross or halo or on a banner with a red cross against a white background, which symbolized the resurrection.

DOVE

In the Christian tradition, the dove appears in the story of Noah and the flood and symbolizes purity, fidelity and peace. It brought back an olive branch which informed Noah that the deluge was over and that there was land on which to begin the new world. Floods are used in many mythologies to symbolize transformation through dissolution in water.

Doves were used in sacrificial ceremonies in early Christian times. Mary offered two doves in sacrifice following the birth of Jesus (Luke 2:24). A dove descended to Jesus Christ after his baptism by John the Baptist, symbolizing divinity, once again confirming, as with all winged creatures, the association with spirituality and Heavenly connection.

THE TRINITY

Christians believe that there is one God made up of three distinct aspects: God the Father, God the son Jesus Christ and God the Holy Ghost or Spirit. The Trinity represents the threefold nature of God. In Ireland, St Patrick used the shamrock to demonstrate the concept that, though there are three separate aspects of God, they are inextricably linked and together make up the whole.

The triqueta is a geometric symbol made up of three interlocking arcs which form a triangle at its centre symbolizing the Trinity, while the complete symbol represents eternity.

Freemasonry

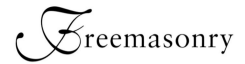

T he origins of Freemasonry lie in France
in the medieval Order of Poor Soldiers
of Christ and Solomon's Temple, usually
known as the Knights Templar. The original
order was given land on the Temple Mount
in Jerusalem and rapidly acquired great
wealth. How this happened is veiled in
mystery, but the Knights Templar went on to
introduce a system of international money
transference – banking – which further
enriched them, financially.

A CRAFTSMEN'S GUILD

The founder of modern Freemasonry, William
Schaw of Saucie, was made King James of
Scotland's Master of Works in 1568. He
oversaw the maintenance and repair of the
royal buildings as well as the construction of
new palaces, castles and hunting lodges. Those
stonemasons who were initiated into the
brotherhood were introduced to the esoteric
Freemason symbols related to building and to
the tools and materials used in construction.
They were also given a mason's mark, their
personal symbolic signature. Masons' marks
are found in many monasteries, palaces and
state buildings such as Westminster Cathedral,
and Roslyn Chapel in Great Britain.

In the late 17th century this association of
workers in stone expanded its membership to
include non-masons. By the 18th century there
were more non-masons than stonemasons in
the membership and Freemasonry was no
longer a true craftsmen's guild.

RELATIONSHIP TO GOD

The symbols used in Masonic rites are based
on the art of building and are used to teach
morals and ethics, and to help the Mason
develop a closer relationship with God or, in
Masonic terms, the 'Grand Architect of the
World'. Indeed, Masons are obliged to honour
a Supreme Power, and the Bible is always
present on the Masonic altar.

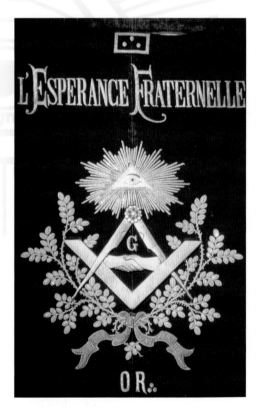

*This illustration from the Masonic Grand Lodge
of France shows the set square and compass.*

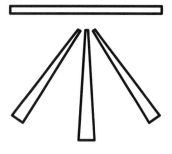

SET SQUARE AND COMPASS

The square is a symbol of morality and was originally drawn as a true carpenter's square, or 'trying' square, with one leg longer than the other. It was a measure for testing or 'trying' the accuracy of the edges of bricks and stones.

The compass is a symbol of virtue. Together, the square and compass have come to symbolize Freemasonry. They are often shown with a letter 'G' in the middle, which is said to stand either for 'God' or 'geometry', as God is regarded as the Grand Architect.

MASON'S MARK OR SIGNATURE

From the 14th century when stonemasons began to become organized, they started leaving their mark or signature on the edifices they built. When a stonemason became a fellowcraft or journeyman, he would select a mark or design that was his for life and could not be changed. It was his trademark and identified him with the building and the quality of his workmanship. These marks were given at a solemn ritual with six master stonemasons present, and at the end of the ceremony the name of the fellowcraft and his mark were entered into a book. The stonemason's mark symbolized their character, integrity and skills and is still used today on letters and documents.

TRIANGLE

In the design of Britain's Neoclassical city of Bath, architect John Wood not only incorporated Masonic imagery into the façades of the houses on his grand street, the Circus, but the plan of the streetscape itself forms a Masonic symbol. If a line is drawn between the three roads that enter the Circus, an equilateral triangle is produced which signifies the Holy Trinity. The triangle itself is set within a circle (formed by the Circus) which is a symbol of eternity.

BLAZING STAR

The Freemason five-pointed star derived from the Pythagoreans' pentagram is the symbol of light, the mystic centre and the expanding universe. Set between square and compasses, representing Heaven and Earth, it stands for the regenerated individual blazing in illumination in a dark unknowing world. It is a symbol of perfection and the divine principle in the initiate's heart.

BLAZING SUN

Masonic symbolism is found as a decorative feature on many buildings. Set squares and compasses are very common, as is a blazing Sun, symbolic of the universe and eternity.

OUROBOROS

The *ouroboros*, an image of a serpent swallowing its own tail, which is a symbol found in many cultures, is another Masonic symbol of eternity, renewal, love and wisdom and can be found on façades, altarpieces and even incorporated into floors and ceilings.

EYE IN A TRIANGLE

An eye inside a triangle symbolizes the ability to see all things and to watch over all matters. This all-seeing eye represents spiritual insight, higher knowledge and the ability to see into occult mysteries. A single unlidded eye symbolizes Divine Essence and Divine Knowledge and, placed within a triangle, it is both a Christian and Masonic symbol. The eye with a triangle in Christian symbolism represents the Holy Trinity. The eye in the top of a triangle is a Masonic mystical sign for the all-knowing God.

WINDING STAIRS

Winding stairs, known as *cochleus* in Scottish Freemasonry, symbolize the progression of the initiate and the stops he must make along the way to reflect on what he has been taught. Similarly, the ladder is a symbol of advancement through the hierarchy. The First Degree ladder has three rungs representing faith, hope and charity. At a more advanced level it has seven rungs which symbolize justice, kindness, good faith, labour, patience and intelligence.

IMMOVABLE JEWELS

In the American system of Freemasonry, the square, the level and the plumb are known as the 'Immovable Jewels of the Lodge'. They are placed in special positions within the lodge: the square to the east, the level to the west and the plumb to the south. In the English system, the Immovable Jewels are the Rough Ashlar, the Perfect Ashlar and the tracing board. These building tools no longer represent physical building and now stand for psychological and spiritual growth.

GREAT SEAL

The Great Seal of the United States is the sacred emblem of the ancient initiates and shows 13 stars, which represent the original states. The eagle symbol holds an olive branch in its right talon with 13 leaves and 13 berries and in its left talon it holds a sheaf of 13 arrows. The olive branch and arrows denote the power of peace and war vested in Congress. The pyramid signifies strength and duration and the eye over it alludes to America's providence.

Gnosticism and Rosicrucianism

The term Gnostic comes from the Greek word *gnosis* meaning 'knowledge'. This knowledge is gained through a process of experiencing, reflecting and using intuition to know oneself and, in the process, discover higher spiritual truth.

The Gnostic Gospels were not discovered as a complete book – but a substantial find, now called the *Nag Hammadi Library*, was made by Egyptian farmers near the town of Nag Hammadi in 1945. Earlier codices, some referring to Mary Magdalene, were found in 1896 and published in 1955.

Gnostic philosophy is believed to have originated in pre-Christian times. Some Gnostics did not call themselves Christians, but others claimed they were the original Christians, a claim that gained greater credence when fragments of Gnostic texts were examined and found to be older than existing Christian gospels.

Gnostics believe that Christ was not truly human, but an avatar or messenger who came in the guise of a human being. The serpent in Gnostic literature is the wisest creature in Paradise because he allowed humans to awaken to higher knowledge.

ROSICRUCIANISM

Rosicrucianism was a secret society that flourished in the 17th and 18th centuries in Europe. Some of its philosophy stems from the Mystery Schools of Ancient Egypt and involves material and spiritual alchemy, metaphysics, sacred architecture, meditation, symbolism, healing mystical practices and the psychic body.

The name means 'rosy cross' and the movement was believed to have been launched after a pamphlet, written by a mythical knight named Christian Rosenkreuz, was found in 1614. The Rosy Cross was used esoterically by the Rosicrucians to symbolize the blood Christ lost on the cross. The seven levels of initiation are represented in the seven rows of seven petals that form the flower. The central rose represents the heart of Christ, divine light, and the Sun at the centre of the wheel of life.

The Modern Rosicrucian Order, called the Ancient Mystical Order Rosea Crucis (AMORC), was founded in 1915 by Harvey Spencer Lewis. With members across the world, it promotes mystical, educational and humanitarian values without allegiance to any religion. There is a special AMORC alphabet and many significant symbols, including the Seal of the Great Master and the Seal of the Supreme Secretary.

The first Rosicrucians in America fled there from persecution in Europe in 1694. Napoleon Bonaparte, emperor of France, was Master of a Parisian Rosicrucian Order and wore the ceremonial collar decorated with the rosy cross.

An example of the alphabet of the Ancient Mystical Order Rosea Crucis.

ſolch hatte er allen auch gehört / in ſolcher zier
ſo ſchöne da ligen / das ich ſchier erſtarret / auch
noch nicht wiß / ob es nur alſo geſchnitten / ode
ein Menſch todt hie lig / dan ſie war gantz vnbe
weglich / noch dorffte ich ſie nicht anrühren. Hie
mit wurde ſie wider bedeckt / vnnd der fürhan
fürgezogen, Mir aber war ſie noch als in Augen
noch erſahe ich bald hinder dem Bett ein Taffel
darauff ſtund alſo geſchrieben :

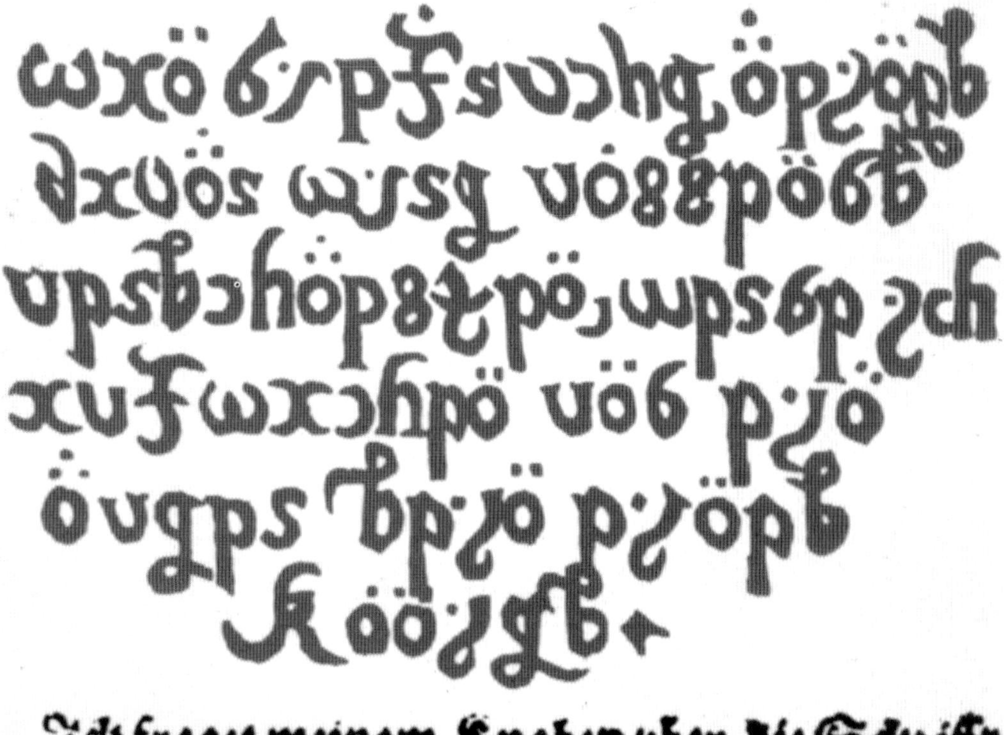

ωχö 6ɾpﬅꙅuꙅhꙅ öꙑö�5b
ꙑxuöꙅ ωɾꙅꙇ vöꙅꙅpöö6ꙅ
vpꙅ6ꙃhöpꙅꙇpö, ωpꙅ6ɾ ꙅch
xuﬅωxꙁhpö vöö pꙑö
öuꙅpꙅ bpꙑö pꙑöpb
Ꙁööꙅꙅꙑb

Ich fraget meinem Knaben vber die Schrifft
Er aber lachet / mit verſprechen / ich ſolte es noch
wol erfahren / Alſo leſchet er die Fackel auß / vnd

```
A B R A C A D A B R A
A B R A C A D A B R
A B R A C A D A B
A B R A C A D A
A B R A C A D
A B R A C A
A B R A C
A B R A
A B R
A B
A
```

ABRACADABRA

This was originally a magical incantation used to ward off evil in occult ceremonies of 2nd-century Gnostics in the Middle East. The word was written on a piece of paper, folded and worn as an amulet for nine days, then just before dawn it was ritually thrown backwards into a stream flowing east. The word comes from a Hebrew word for the Trinity. Abracadabra was written in an inverted triangle.

ABRAXAS

The god Abraxas or Anguipede has a human body topped with the head of a cockerel and legs of snakes. It is the symbol of Pantheus, all gods in one. Abraxas is found in Greek mythology, but was also mentioned in Gnostic texts such as the *Gospel of the Egyptians*.

OUROBOROS

The 'World Serpent', as the Gnostics called the snake swallowing its tail, symbolized humanity being ensnared by the Earth, locked in a system that prevents divine connection. The snake was an important symbol for the Gnostics, particularly the Naassene sect, whose name derives from *naass*, meaning 'snake'. Some Gnostic rites included serpents as part of the ceremony.

ROSICRUCIAN ROSE

For Rosicrucians the way in which a rose
blossoms by unfolding symbolizes the gradual
unfolding of spirituality. The colour red
symbolizes the blood of Christ, and the golden
heart concealed at the centre of the rose
represents the spiritual gold at the heart of
human nature. The rose symbolizes the heart,
which has been used to symbolize love and
compassion throughout spiritual practices.

CRUCIFIED ROSE

This was the original symbol of the
Rosicrucian Fraternity; in it a hieroglyphic
rose is crucified in the centre of a cross.
The layers of petals represent the stages
of initiation and the very centre symbolizes
unity with Christ.

GOLDEN AND ROSY CROSS

This symbolizes spiritual gold and is worn as
an insignia by Rosicrucians. It often bears
the alchemical symbols of salt, sulphur and
mercury, a star and the words faith, hope,
love and patience. The Rosicrucian initiate
could not reach the adept level until he had
transmuted his base metal of ignorance into
the pure gold of wisdom and understanding
through rituals, rites and learning the secrets
of the brotherhood.

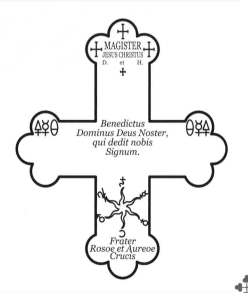

Islam

The five pillars of Islam represent the five main beliefs of Muslims: belief in Allah and the teachings of the Prophet Mohammed (*Shahadah*); ritual prayer five times a day (*Salat*); almsgiving (*Zakat*); fasting (*Ramadan*); and pilgrimage to Mecca once in a lifetime (*Hajj*). The pillars symbolize support for the beliefs that must be translated into everyday behaviour and actions. In Islam religious practice is part of all aspects of life and there is no separation between the religious and the secular.

ISLAMIC ARCHITECTURE

In Islamic architecture, in the mosques, palaces, schools and forts, we see symbols of power. The caravanserai or caravan inns, such as the Madarshah caravanserai in Isfahan, Iran that housed the camel traders on their journeys across the empire, reflect the importance of the Islamic trading empire and are some of the most impressive buildings in the Islamic style.

Islamic architecture is divided into religious and secular. Islamic mosques characteristically have large domes that symbolize the sky, the universe and creation – in fact, the mosque in its entirety is a symbol of the world. From the minaret or tower the muezzin calls the faithful to prayer and the large courtyards often hold a central prayer hall. The word 'minaret' comes from the Arabic *minara*, meaning 'giving of light'. It symbolizes spiritual illumination through prayer and the worship of Allah.

DECORATION AND DESIGN

Early Islam prohibited the depiction of the human form and the natural world and still prohibits depiction of the Prophet today. Subsequently, calligraphy and the arabesque were used to express the ideals of nature.

Extensive use of decorative Arabic calligraphy using quotations from the Qur'an covers the walls of mosques. Fountains provide water for washing before prayers, and bright colours are used throughout. The Alhambra in Granada, in Spain, with its interior spaces decorated in arabesques and colours of red, blue and gold, epitomizes the beauty of Islamic architecture built to inspire awe and wonderment in veneration of Allah. The Taj Mahal at Agra in India is one of the most beautiful examples of a mausoleum.

Islamic architecture is decorated with intricate, exquisite calligraphy and arabesques.

ARABESQUE

The arabesque is a highly complex, repeated motif which represents the journey to the sublime. The linear style is based on flowers, leaves and tendrils that intertwine and are an aid to meditation. The arabesque is seen not as a pattern, but as a rhythm or an incantation that repeats the motif endlessly. It has no beginning or end and symbolizes Allah who is limitless. Symbolically, arabesques are linked to the Qur'anic evocation of Paradise as a glorious, verdant garden. Early Islam prohibited the painting of the human form and so calligraphy and the arabesque evolved to express the ideals of order and nature.

STAR AND CRESCENT

The crescent in Islam represents divine authority and increase because of its association with the crescent Moon. It also represents the expansion of the Islamic world. The morning star represents Paradise. Together the star and crescent are the emblem of the Islamic world, featuring prominently on Islamic flags, including those of Pakistan and Turkey. The joint symbol was adopted from the Ottoman Empire, which saw the celestial bodies as symbolic of God's nature. Crescents and stars feature on Islamic coins, banners, textiles and in architecture.

KAABA

The Kaaba, 'the Sacred House', is located within the Great Mosque at Mecca and is the most important sacred shrine in Islam. Entry is forbidden to non-Muslims. The Kaaba is a simple, cube-shaped stone building which is at the centre of the courtyard and is believed to have been the first building erected for the worship of Allah and symbolizes his presence amongst the faithful. Muslims pray five times a day facing the Kaaba in Mecca.

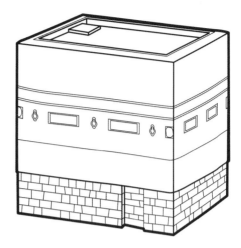

In the eastern corner of the Kaaba is the Black Stone, which is thought to be a meteorite remnant, the symbol of divine power and divinity given directly from Heaven and symbolizing communication between man and God. The entire Kaaba is covered with a black silk cloth, since looking directly at it is considered as disrespectful as looking directly into the face of Allah. Pilgrims circle the Kaaba seven times, which symbolize the seven attributes of God.

TREE OF LIFE

As in other religious traditions, the Tree of Life in Islam represents the connection between the Underworld, Earth and Paradise. It also symbolizes abundance and plenty. In the Qur'an, Mohammed is described as seeing the Tree of Tuba in the middle of Paradise. It was dazzling with emeralds, sapphires and rubies among its branches as milk and honey sprang from its roots.

ZULFIQAR

Shi'ite Muslims believe that Mohammed carried a sword called Zulfiqar, which he passed on to his son-in-law and cousin Ali ibn Abi Talib, a renowned warrior. Zulfiqar came to symbolize both the inheritance of power and authority from Mohammed and Ali's great bravery.

HAND OF FATIMA

The hand of Fatima is the symbol of temporal and spiritual power, strength, protection and domination. In Islam, the open hand of Fatima, with five fingers held upwards, symbolizes the five fundamentals of the Islamic religion – faith, prayer, pilgrimage, fasting and charity. The thumb represents the Prophet, the first finger is Lady Fatima, the second her husband Ali, and the remaining two fingers, their sons Hasan and Husain.

Fatima was the daughter of Mohammed and Aisha, and to Shi'ite Muslims has a similar status to the Virgin Mary. She is known as 'Pure and Holy' and the 'Mistress of the Women of the World'. Shi'ite women travel to shrines dedicated to Fatima, where they seek her help. Amulets of the 'Hand of Fatima', frequently highly decorative and made from metal, are sacred symbols which are hung on walls or worn for protection.

COLOURS

The Islamic tradition is rich in colour symbolism and is tinged with magical beliefs. Black is used as a charm against the evil eye. It is the colour of mourning and the colour of the chador worn by devout Muslim women. White is thought of as lucky and symbolizes purity and peace, and many Muslims wear white when they attend Friday prayers. According to the poet and mystic Rumi, to reach the absolute Light through mystical practices is to rise through blue, red, yellow, white, green and pale blue until one reaches the colourless light.

The colour green has long been associated with Islam and it represents plant life and fertility. Mohammed wore a green cloak and turban and the colour symbolizes nature and life and the physical manifestation of God. In the Qur'an, Surah 18:31, it says that the inhabitants of Paradise will wear green garments of fine silk. The colour was associated with Islam even at the time of the Crusades, when Crusaders avoided using any green in their clothes lest they be mistaken for their Muslim opponents in the chaos of battle.

Muslim women at prayer often wear white, which symbolizes purity and peace.

RELIGIOUS SYMBOLS: EASTERN

Symbolism in Eastern religious traditions is included in all aspects of devotion and can be found in music, in images of the deities, in rituals and even in symbolic hand gestures used in sacred dance. There is much overlap in Eastern symbolism, though Hinduism, Buddhism and Taoism have symbols unique to their own practice.

Hinduism, the oldest living religion, is replete with symbolism, including sounds, foods and colours as well as a panoply of sacred images. Hinduism developed from the Vedic religion. The four ancient Vedas provide guidance on philosophy, reincarnation, karma, and sacred songs and rituals to be performed to worship the many Hindu deities who are the manifestation of the Supreme Cosmic Spirit, Brahman.

In Tibetan Buddhism, symbolism plays a significant part in meditation and prayer. Chants and musical instruments are used and monks take part in sacred processions and rituals. Through ritual and meditation, the devotee invokes powerful deities and visualizes their presence to request their help in removing obstacles on the path to spiritual enlightenment.

Taoism or Daoism is based on the ancient work *Tao-T-Ching,* the *I Ching, Book of Changes,* which was written sometime between 300 BCE and 600 BCE and is attributed to the philosopher Lao Tse. Taoism is the natural order and force that flows through all beings. Tao is not so much a deity as a way of being in which equilibrium is the state to be achieved.

Hinduism

The Hindu deities symbolize the forces of nature as well as those within humans. They represent cosmic powers and human vices and virtues. All Hindu deities are symbols of the Absolute and represent a particular facet of Brahman, the Supreme Cosmic Spirit. The Hindu trinity is represented by three major gods: Brahma, the creator and agent of Brahman; Vishnu, the protector; and Shiva, the destroyer. The gods are represented symbolically by icons called *murtiti*.

ATTRIBUTES OF THE GODS

Hindus can choose any of the major or minor deities to worship according to their needs. Each of the gods has special symbols associated with them. Brahma carries the sacred texts, the Vedas, which symbolize his supreme power over creative and religious knowledge. The five-pointed star is the emblem of Shiva, who is sometimes depicted with five faces. Shiva is almost always worshipped as a pillar-like stone called a lingam, which represents the penis. Vishnu carries the rayed disc, a solar symbol, which represents his absolute power to destroy as well as create. He is also shown with the conch which stands for the five elements and eternity.

The gods are associated with the 'vehicles' that carry them. Ganesh, the elephant god, is carried by a mouse, which represents the feelings of timidity that may overwhelm us when we start a new venture; the blessing of Ganesh can help overcome this. Vishnu rides on a serpent which represents the desire for consciousness, while Shiva rides the Nandi bull, a symbol of brute strength as well as unbridled sexuality, which only he can help to control. Vishnu's consort, Kali, rides a lion, symbolizing her anger, pride and mercilessness, qualities that her devotees would pray to diminish in themselves by worshipping her.

RITUALS AND SHRINES

In Vedic rituals, such as puja, ceremonial offerings are made to the deity. Every gift and every object that is connected to the puja has symbolic significance. The statue or *vigraha*, the image of the deity, signifies purity. The flower that is offered symbolizes the good that has grown or blossomed in the devotee. Fruit symbolizes detachment, surrender and self-sacrifice. The lighted lamp signifies the illumination in the soul and red or vermilion powder scattered at the shrine represents the emotions of the worshipper.

Hindu temples have their principal shrine facing the rising Sun and their entrance facing east. The temple design reinforces the idea that life goes from the temporal realm to the eternal one.

Together the yoni and lingam symbolize procreation and the source of life.

Principal Gods in the Hindu Pantheon

There are many gods within Hindu culture and religious practice, and even the principal gods are represented in various forms. The members of the *trimurti* or trinity are Brahma, Vishnu and Shiva.

BRAHMA

The creator god, Brahma, one of the three *trimurti*, is lord of the gods and humanity. He created the cosmos and is usually depicted as having four heads and hands. His four heads represent the four directions. In his hands he carries a sacrificial tool, the Vedas (holy scriptures), a water pot and prayer beads. He is the intermediary between Vishnu and Shiva.

SHIVA

The lord of destruction and renewal, Shiva is one of the Hindu trinity. He is a god of opposites and is associated with the erotic. He is the god of masculinity and is often shown riding the bull, Nandi, symbol of virility. He is depicted with a third eye in the middle of his forehead to symbolise enlightenment. Shiva is also known as Lord of the Dance.

VISHNU

Vishnu is the preserver of the cosmos, the protector of the world. He appears as many avatars when the world is under threat, such as Rama and Krishna, in human form, and as Kurma, a tortoise, Matsya, a fish, and many more forms. He carries a conch shell, to chase away demons, a club, indicating his strength, a discus, to use against evil, and a lotus, symbolizing reincarnation.

KRISHNA

Lord Krishna is the eighth incarnation of Vishnu and is known as the divine cow herder. In his youth, when he herded cows, he played his flute to attract the wives and daughters of cowherds, which is why he became known as a great lover and is associated with the joyful relationship between the gods and humans. He is known for his wild pranks and playful nature.

GANESH

Also called Ganesha, this elephant-headed deity is known for his ability to overcome all obstacles. He symbolizes abundance and sacred knowledge and is seen as the bringer of joy to families. Ganesh's head represents both wisdom and the soul, or *Atman*, the ultimate divinity humans may achieve. His human body, *Maya*, represents the earthly existence of humanity.

KALI

A feminine form of the divine, Kali portrays destructive energy, but is also a mother goddess linked with creation. Known as the Dark Mother, Kali carries a sword and the head of a devil she has killed and wears a necklace of 50 skulls. These skulls represent the 50 characters of the Sanskrit alphabet and indicate Kali's role as the goddess of knowledge and the destroyer of ignorance.

Lesser Gods

Hindu gods and goddesses present different forms or aspects of the same god or divine energy. These are a few of the best-known aspects of the major gods.

PARVATI

Energy of Shiva

LAKSHMI

Energy of Vishnu

HANUMAN

Monkey-god

VARUNA

God of sky, rain and celestial ocean

INDRA

King of gods, ruler of Heavens

VAYU

Friend and servant
of Indra

SURYA

Chief solar deity

YAMA

God of death

LINGAM

The word 'lingam' is derived from a Sanskrit root *langala*, which means 'plough' or 'phallus', and is the symbol of procreation and the source of life. The lingam represents Shiva, the creator, cosmic energy and the renewal of life.

LINGAM

YONI

YONI

The Hindu symbol for the vulva or womb. It symbolizes the feminine, receptive and passive principle and links to the lingam as the male principle.

PURNAKUMBHA

The Purnakumbha, a ceremonial earthenware pot filled with water, is used prior to the start of puja and is placed before the most important deity. It symbolizes Mother Earth, the water life-giver.

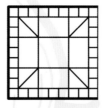

MANDALA

The traditional Hindu mandala is a square divided into smaller squares. This also forms the basic layout for Hindu temples. The central square is the Place of Brahma and holds the 'womb chamber', the holiest part of the temple where the altar is situated.

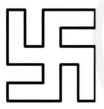

SWASTIKA

The word 'swastika' is a combination of two Sanskrit words, *su* meaning 'well' and *astai* meaning 'being', and is interpreted as 'may good prevail', both in personal and universal terms. It represents a positive life force and joy, and the eternal nature of Brahman because it points in all directions, symbolizing his omnipresence. In all traditions the swastika was a very positive symbol until its meaning was sullied by association with the Nazis.

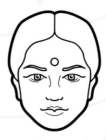

TILAKA

The tilaka is a symbolic mark on the forehead or between the eyes in the position of the third eye. It symbolizes the need to cultivate super-consciousness in order to open up the mystical third eye. The tilaka itself, and the occasions on which it is worn, varies according to the branch of Hinduism that the devotee follows or their marital status. It is most commonly seen in the decorative dot, the bindi.

OM

This Sanskrit symbol for the sacred Hindu sound OM (aum) is known as the mother of all mantras. It is the most important symbol in Hinduism. The whole cosmos stems from the vibration of the sound Om in Hindu cosmology. The four parts of the sound symbolize four stages of consciousness: awake, asleep, dreaming and trance or the state of transcendence. This mystic sound is so important that no sacred event would take place without it. It begins every Hindu prayer and invocation and is found in every Hindu temple and family shrine. It is a sacred symbol that represents Brahman, the Supreme Divinity, the fount of all existence who is unknowable. Om represents the whole universe and is so sacred it must only be uttered with complete attention.

SHRI-YANTRA

The yantra is a form of mandala that means 'instrument' and is made up of nine linked triangles. It symbolizes the play of cosmic forces and creation. The shri-yantra, a highly sacred symbol, is used in Hindu tantric ritual. The central part features upward-pointing triangles which represent the lingam or phallus, and downward-pointing triangles which represent the yoni, vulva or womb. It symbolizes the sexual union of the gods Shakti and Shiva. At the centre of other mandalas there is a triangle with a bindi (a dot), inside a circle which symbolizes the merging of male and female forces.

TRISULA

This is a tri-headed spear or trident associated with the Lord Shiva – the goddess Shakti also carries the trident. The three prongs are said to represent various trinities, including the three powers or *shaktis*: will, action and wisdom; creation, maintenance and destruction; past, present and future.

GARUDA

Ridden by Vishnu, Garuda has the body of a bird of prey, a human head with three eyes and an eagle's beak. It is often shown tearing serpents apart and symbolizes the endless fight between good and evil, life and death, and Heavenly powers against Earthly matters. The strength of the symbol is doubled in the presence of Vishnu as he is the god who destroys life and restores it.

Buddhism

Siddhartha Gautama was a prince of the Sakya clan in Lumbini, Nepal, *c.*500 BCE. Raised in luxury, he first learned about sickness and death as he rode outside his palace and saw the suffering of others. At the age of 29 he abandoned his princely life and devoted himself to finding a way of being free of the endless cycle of birth, death and rebirth.

After seven years of searching for enlightenment, he decided to sit under the Bodhi tree until he resolved the problem of suffering on Earth. Though he was taunted and tempted by the god of death, Mara, on the 49th day he attained enlightenment and became known as Buddha, the Awakened One. Although he had achieved Nirvana, a state of perfect peace, he decided to stay in the earthly realm to teach others the way to enlightenment.

ANICONIC SYMBOLISM

Early Buddhist symbols of the 3rd century BCE were aniconic; that is, they did not directly depict the Buddha. Symbols included the stupa, Dharma Wheel, swastika and also the lotus flower. In the 1st century CE figurative imagery became more common and the first human representations of the Buddha appeared.

CENTRAL TENETS

The belief in the Middle Way, a path of moderation between the extremes of self-indulgence and self-denial, is an important part of Buddhism. Reincarnation is a central tenet and the Dharma Wheel represents the cycle of birth, death and rebirth, the teachings of the Buddha Dharma and the Noble Eightfold Path, signified by the eight spokes.

The Dharma Wheel represents the way that Buddhist teaching and practice lead to enlightenment.

STUPA

Stupa means summit, and stupas were first built on burial mounds that contained the relics of the Buddha or those of his disciples who had become enlightened. They symbolize the Buddha and his release from *samsara*, the cycle of birth, death and rebirth. The stupa is a cosmic sign made up of a dome that represents the 'world egg', symbol of creation and the womb. The relics represent the seeds of life. Later, stupas became places of worship and were built to mark special events.

MANDALA

Mandala is the Sanskrit word for circle, the symbol of natural wholeness, and mandalas always have a concentric structure even though they may be contained within a square. Mandalas are used in Hindu and Buddhist traditions as an aid to meditation and represent spiritual, cosmic and psychic order.

The design of the mandala, the complex use of geometric patterns, colours and the inclusion of deities in some mandalas all direct the worshipper to the sacred space at the centre which represents the divine presence. In Hindu tradition this is *shunya*, absolute void, and *binhu*, cosmic seed. It symbolizes the belief that from this void everything arose and it is the place to which everything will return. By meditating on this, the worshipper can achieve stillness and separation from the illusions of permanence in the material world. It symbolizes harmony and balance and the journey to enlightenment.

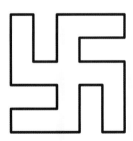

MANJI

The Buddhist 'swastika' is a symbol of good luck. It is known as the *manji*, the sign of a whirlwind, and represents Dharma, the balance of opposites and universal harmony. In Zen Buddhism it represents the harmony between love and intellect.

TRIRATNA/TRISULA

The *triratna* or trident (also known as a trisula) signifies lightning, thunderbolt and the triple flame, which together represent the three weapons of the Heavens. It also symbolizes the Three Jewels of Buddhism, which are Buddha, Dharma or Buddhist teachings, and Sangha or enlightened community.

EYES OF THE BUDDHA

The Buddha is often depicted with a third eye in the centre of his forehead, similar to the Hindu god Shiva. It is the eye of supreme perception and is usually shown as being closed as the Buddha focuses on inner contemplation.

WREATH OF FLAMES

The fire wreath is the symbol of highest consciousness. For Buddhists, fire and flames symbolize wisdom that burns away ignorance. Meditating on a fire wreath in a mandala drives out darkness and helps to open the path to transcendental wisdom.

FOOTPRINT OF THE BUDDHA

The Buddha's footprint, the Buddhapada, symbolizes the teachings of the Buddha and his presence on Earth. It is decorated with symbols important in Buddhism, such as the swastika, conch and wheel. The image of the foot represents following the path of the Buddha.

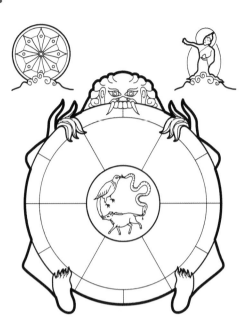

WHEEL OF LIFE

Also known as the Bhavacakra, the wheel of life is held and turned by the jaws, hands and feet of a fearsome figure, who is often depicted as Yama, the Lord of Death. This figure symbolizes the inevitablility of death and the impermanance of attachment. The Wheel of Life's six main sections symbolize the six realms of existence: the worlds of Devas (Gods); Asuras (Demigods, Titans and Fighting Demons); Humans; Animals; Pretas (hungry ghosts); and Hell. The twelve outer sections show the Twelve Links of Causality: ignorance; volitional action; consciousness; name and form; six sensory organs (eye, ear, nose, tongue, body, and mind); contact or touch; sensation; desire, craving; grasping; becoming; birth; decay and death.

THE THREE JEWELS

The 'Three Jewels' are the Buddha, the Dharma or Buddhist teachings, and the Sangha or the community of monks. They are represented by the *triratna*, or *trisula* (see pages 92 and 239).

TRIKONA

The *trikona*, an equilateral triangle, is found on paintings and carvings of the Buddha. It represents the Buddha-Mind, the power to overcome all temptations and symbolizes omniscience. Pointing down it indicates the lingam; pointing up, the yoni; and two *trikonas* forming a star signify creative activity.

The Eight Auspicious Symbols of Buddhism

While many sacred symbols appear in Buddhist art, the most important are the group of eight known in Sanskrit as the *Ashtamangala*, *ashta* meaning 'eight' and *mangala* meaning 'auspicious'. Each of these symbols is also associated with the physical form of the Buddha.

THE VICTORY BANNER

Originally a military standard carried in ancient Indian warfare, the banner was adopted by Buddhism as an emblem of the Buddha's enlightenment, heralding the triumph of knowledge over ignorance. The banner also denotes Buddha's triumph over Mara, who personifies hindrances on the path to spiritual progress.

THE GOLDEN FISHES

A pair of fish was originally an ancient symbol of the two sacred rivers of India, the Ganga and Yamuna. In Buddhism fish signify happiness as they have total freedom in the water. They also represent fertility and abundance because they multiply rapidly. Because fish often swim in pairs, in China they represent conjugal unity and fidelity.

THE ENDLESS KNOT

Some speculate that the endless knot evolved from an ancient Indian symbol of the Naga or cobra, showing two stylized snakes intertwined with one another. The intertwining lines of the knot symbolize the way in which all phenomena are linked by cause and effect, and thus the knot represents karma. As the knot has no beginning or end it also represents the infinite wisdom of the Buddha.

THE TREASURE VASE

In traditional art, the treasure vase is shown as a round vessel with a short neck. On the top at its opening is a large jewel to reflect the fact that it holds treasure. Wealth vases, sealed with precious and sacred substances, are still commonly placed on altars on mountain passes, where they are believed to attract wealth and bring harmony to the environment. The treasure vase represents the spiritual abundance of the Buddha.

THE CONCH SHELL

Originally a trumpet used in ancient Indian warfare, in Buddhism the conch represents the fame of Buddha's teaching spreading in all directions like the sound of the trumpet. In Tibetan Buddhism a conch shell is used to call together religious assemblies and also functions as a ritual musical instrument and a container for holy water. Shells which spiral to the right in a clockwise direction are considered especially sacred and are believed to echo the celestial motion of the Sun, Moon and planets. In statues and images of the Buddha, the conch appears at his throat. It also appears as an auspicious mark on the soles, palms, limbs, breast or forehead of a divinely endowed being.

THE WHEEL

The wheel consists of three parts: the hub, the rim and the spokes. The circle represents the perfection and completeness of the teaching of Buddha. More specifically, the rim represents the limitation of our actions in the world, the hub represents the axis of the world and the eight spokes represent the eightfold path to enlightenment. The wheel's swift motion also symbolizes the rapid spiritual changes brought about by the teaching of the Buddha.

THE LOTUS

The lotus symbolizes the progress of the soul towards enlightenment. This is reflected in the growth of the plant, which has its roots in mud, representing materialism, its stem rising through the waters of experience, and its flower basking in the sunshine of enlightenment. In many paintings and sculptures the Buddha is shown sitting on a lotus flower. According to an ancient manuscript, 'the heart of men is like an unopened lotus: when the virtues of the Buddha develop therein, the lotus blossoms; that is why the Buddha sits on a lotus bloom.'

THE PARASOL

The traditional Indian parasol offers protection from the heat of the Sun. In Buddhist terms this has come to mean protection from the heat of suffering, desire and other spiritually harmful forces. It also symbolizes honour and respect. The dome of the umbrella is held aloft by a vertical handle that represents the axis holding up the world. During processions an umbrella is carried above an important person or image of a deity to signify that the person or symbol below is the centre of the universe. Depictions of the Buddha often show a large umbrella above his head.

The Eight Symbols of Happiness

The Eight Lucky Articles or Bringers of Good Fortune represent aspects of the Eightfold Noble Path and support the Buddhist follower in their practice to reach enlightenment.

PRECIOUS MEDICINE

Precious Medicine, *ghi-wang*, means 'cow essence'. It is a calming and strengthening medicine which is drawn from the gallstones of cattle or elephants. Just as the medicine is used to remedy physical suffering, so suffering is part of the practice of Dharma. It symbolizes Right Mindfulness, which combats ignorance and the suffering it brings.

BAEL FRUIT

Also known as Wood Apple or Bilva Fruit, this represents the emptiness and the dependent nature of existence. It contains healing properties and aids in the treatment of digestive diseases. It signifies Right Action which bears the right fruit.

MUSTARD SEEDS

White Mustard Seeds represent the story of the woman whose child had died. Utterly distressed she came to the Buddha, who told her to go into every home and bring back mustard seed from any that had not had a bereavement. When she returned empty-handed he showed she was not alone in her grief and that death was an unavoidable part of life. It signifies Right Understanding.

CLOCKWISE-SPIRALLED CONCH SHELL

The right-spiralling conch shell is seen as particularly sacred. It symbolizes the Buddha's voice, calling his followers to prayer, and his teachings that spread in all directions, like the sound of the shell when it is used as a horn or bugle. It stands for Right Speech.

MIRROR

The Mirror represents the Dharmakaya, the Truth Body of the Buddha, and the purity and wisdom contained within. A mirror is clear and unsullied and reflects all without judgement, encouraging better understanding. It also symbolizes Right Thought.

CINNABAR

Cinnabar and vermilion are red powders and in Tantric Buddhist colour symbolism, red represents control. It signifies that control which is needed to follow the teachings and discipline of meditation in order to gain enlightenment. It represents Right Concentration.

YOGURT

Sometimes called Curd, this pure white food is the result of a long process and symbolizes the practice of Buddhism which takes place over time, during which impurities of mind are removed. It represents Right Livelihood as no animals are hurt in the production of Yogurt.

DURVA GRASS

Durva Grass is strong, resistant to disease and long lasting. It symbolizes long life ,which gives the Buddhist practitioner time to follow the teachings and attain enlightenment. It signifies Right Effort.

The Mudras

Images of the Buddha display characteristic hand gestures called *mudras*, which have a well-defined, fixed meaning. These are just a few of the many *mudras*, each with its own particular meaning and symbolism.

DHARMACHAKRA MUDRA

The gesture of teaching shows the Buddha with both hands held level with the heart and the thumbs and index fingers forming circles. It is interpreted as turning the Wheel of Dharma.

VARADA MUDRA

The gesture of charity and compassion, this shows the lowered left hand with the palm turned outwards. The fingers represent generosity, morality, patience, effort and meditative concentration.

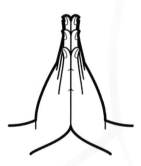

NAMASKARA MUDRA

The gesture of greeting, prayer and adoration in which the palms are pressed together with the fingers pointing upwards. Buddhas no longer make this gesture since they do not have to show devotion to anything.

ABHAYA MUDRA

The gesture of protection and dispelling of fear, also known as the gesture of blessing and reassurance, it has the right hand slightly elevated, with the open palm facing outwards.

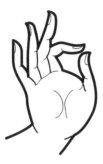

TARJANI MUDRA

The gesture of warning or threat, or warding off evil, has the forefinger and little finger outstretched.

VITARKA MUDRA

The gesture of discussion and debate, in which the teachings of the Buddha are explained, has hands raised and the tips of the forefingers and thumbs touching.

BUDDHA-SHRAMANA MUDRA

The gesture beyond misery shows the hand palm upwards with outstretched fingers. It is also called an ascetic's gesture of renunciation.

BHUTADAMARA MUDRA

The gesture of warding off the evil eye, with hands raised, backs of the hands touching and some fingers curled towards the palm, is the gesture of protection.

DHYANA MUDRA

The gesture of meditation, with both hands resting on the Buddha's lap, right hand above the left hand with palms facing upwards. It is the position used by yogis during meditation and the gesture of absolute balance.

Taoism

Some scholars believe that Taoism originated in China as early as the Ice Age, when shamans, who also practised divination, harnessed cosmic powers to fly, in order to access other worlds. The main shaman was King Fu Xi, who is believed to have lived about 2800 BCE, although some think he is a mythical character.

THE TAO TE CHING

Taoism began in earnest with Lao Tzu in the 3rd or 4th century BCE. He is said to have had 13 incarnations, starting in the reign of Fu Xi, and is the reputed author of the *Tao Te Ching*, which can be translated as *The Book of the Way and its Virtue*, which is fundamental to the Taoist school of Chinese philosophy.

Taoism taught that the universe is governed by *Tao*, the Way – cosmic energy compounded in yin, representing the female, negative principle and yang, the male, positive energy. All creation, including human beings, is a product of these forces. By understanding our own nature we can then understand the universe. Taoist tradition fostered many magical practices and mysticism as a way of influencing cosmic forces.

THE I CHING

Another seminal Taoist text is the *I Ching, Book of Changes*. It is a form of oracle which guides those who seek its ancient wisdom. Taoist roots go back to 3000 BCE and are founded on the concept of the unity of man and the cosmos and the complementary nature of yin and yang energy. Combinations of eight trigrams, *pakua*, comprise 64 hexagrams which are alternately celestial and terrestrial. The trigrams symbolize the Taoist belief that the universe is in a constant state of flux between yin and yang. Fortune telling, divination, astrology and palmistry are traditional Taoist activities.

The ceiling of this theatre in Jiayuguan, China, shows the pakua, *an octagonal diagram with one trigram on each side, which is used in Feng Shui.*

P'AN-KU

In Chinese mythology the giant P'an-ku is the creator of mankind. He emerged from the cosmic hen's egg that existed before Heaven and Earth were created. When the egg divided, yin and yang appeared. For 18,000 years he laboured to fill the space between Heaven and Earth, which had separated, and put the Sun, Moon, stars and planets in their orbits. When he died his body became all the natural elements that make up the Earth.

YIN AND YANG

Yin and yang represent the fusion of two cosmic forces into one whole, known as the *taiji* (tai-chi). It is symbolized by a circle divided by a curved line into one dark side, yin, which symbolizes darkness and female energy, and a white side, which symbolizes lightness and masculine energy. Each half carries the seed of the other, a dark dot on the light side and a light dot on the dark side. Their interdependence signifies balanced movement of opposites. It symbolizes the Tao desire to achieve perfect balance between contrary principles.

SHOU-LAO

Shou-lao is the Chinese character for long life and is often found on ceramics, in statue form and in textiles. He is sometimes depicted as an old man with a peach or a figure within the fruit. The peach is the symbol of female genitalia and is connected with Taoist sexual mysticism, so Shou-lao is associated with mystic sexual practices that prolong life. Peach blossom in Taoism is the symbol of a virgin and was the yonic source of life.

I Ching Trigrams

The *I Ching* communicates through 64 hexagrams, which create questions for the oracle. These are made up of a combination of two of eight possible trigrams, each symbolizing many things.

CHIEN
The Creative. Represents yang and the patriarch. Its element is big metal and its animal is the horse, denoting power, endurance and strength.

KUN
The Receptive. Represents yin and the mother. Its element is big earth and its animal a cow with calf, denoting family, docility and submission.

CHEN
The Arousing. Represents the eldest son, decision-making, movement and growth. Its element is big wood and its animal the dragon.

SUN
The Penetrating. Represents the eldest daughter and wind. Its element is small wood and its animal the rooster, a bird of opportunity and reliability.

TUI
The Joyous. Represents the youngest daughter, happiness and a celebration. Its element is small metal. It advocates turning away from worry.

KEN
The Mountain. Represents the youngest son, mystery and hidden expectations. Its element is small earth and it is linked to death and new beginnings.

KAN
The Abysmal. Represents the middle son, danger and warnings. Its element is water, its season, winter. It symbolizes sadness, hardship and toil.

LI
The Clinging. Represents the middle daughter and dependence. It signifies fire, sun, brightness and warmth and suggests potential.

The Eight Flower Symbols of Taoism

Healthy flowers manifest good Chi and represent growth, fulfillment, new, prosperous beginnings, good fortune and success.

PEONY

The fulsome blossom of the peony symbolizes wealth, dignity and love. It was chosen as the imperial flower of China and represents spring.

LOTUS

This flower represents summer in the symbolism of the four seasons. The Amadist community, a major Taoist secret society founded in 4th-century China, used the white lotus as its emblem.

CHRYSANTHEMUM

The China Astor or *Crysanthemum indicum* is a symbol of happiness. It represents autumn in the symbolism of the four seasons.

PLUM

The hardy plum is one of the first trees to come into blossom in late winter, and it symbolizes longevity and happy marriage. The sage Lao-tse was born under a plum tree. The plum tree was an emblem of the samurai in Japan. It represents winter in the symbolism of the four seasons.

NARCISSUS

The narcissus blooms at the Chinese New Year and is the symbol of joy, good fortune and a happy marriage. A white narcissus was sacred in China.

PEACH

The peach blossom was said to be the main ingredient of the elixir of immortality.

ORCHID

To the Chinese the orchid represents luxury, harmony, refinement and beauty. It symbolizes fertility and is sometimes used as a charm against sterility and to increase potency.

BAMBOO

The bamboo, with the plum and pine, is one the three trees of good omen called 'The Three Friends of Winter'. It is the emblem of the Chinese bodhisattva Guanyin, goddess of mercy. Its straight stem reaching to the sky, the space between the knots in the stem and the hollow centre symbolize the objectives of Taoist meditative practice.

The Eight Emblems of the Immortals

The eight immortals were legendary figures of Taoism who knew all the secrets of nature. The emblems symbolize the individual and would be understood by those who followed the Taoist tradition. The immortals have many attributes, including the ability to make themselves invisible, the power to free those in captivity and to turn stone into gold. Symbols representing the different characteristic emblems of each immortal decorated embroidery, porcelain, bronze and ivory, and blessings were bestowed on anyone who wore the emblems of the immortals.

FAN
This is carried by Zhuang-li Quan along with a peach to revive the souls of the dead. The fan is a symbol of delicate feelings.

FLUTE
Han Xiang-zi and his flute have the power to make flowers grow and blossom. It is also a symbol of harmony.

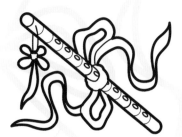

CASTANETS
Cao Gou-Jiu was thought to be the brother of a 10th-century Sung empress and his emblem, the castanets symbolize his free access to the palace and the power of his rank.

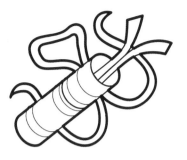

BAMBOO DRUM

The symbol of Zhang Guo-lao is the fish drum and represents old age and longevity.

FLOWER BASKET

This is the symbol of the patron saint of florists and also a symbol of pleasure that is delusional. The female immortal Lan Cai-He carries her emblem, a basket of flowers, which symbolize the transience of life.

SWORD

Lu Dong-bin's emblem is the sword, which symbolises his journeys across the world fighting evil and destroying dragons.

GOURD

The double gourd and the crutch are the symbols of Li Tue-guai and represent his power to free his soul from his body and to help those in the celestial realm. It is said that while away from his body on an astral journey, a follower thought he was dead and burned his body. On his return, Li Tue-guai entered the body of a beggar as he no longer had a body to house his spirit.

LOTUS

The emblem of He Xian gu, one of the two female immortals, is the lotus pod and is supposed to give help in housekeeping.

The Book of Spirits

Saturday ♄ Cassi...
Ro...

Conjuro & confirmo super vos Cassiel, Mi...
Seraquell Angeli fortes & potentis & per n...
Adonai, Adonai, Adonai, Eie, Eie, Ei...
cum Cados, Cados, Ina vel Ima Saclay ...
Domini formatoris Seculorum qui Se...
que ovit & per illum qui in bene pla...
filio Israel in hereditatem observandum...
eum firmeter custodirent & Sanctificarent...
tendendum inde bonam in alio secula ver...
letionem & per nomina Angelorem servie...
exercitu Septimo Booel Angel magno & ...
potenti principi & per nomen Stellum...
et Saturnus & per sanctum sigillum...
& per nomina predicta &c. &c.

See the Conjuration of Saturday i...
ceremonial magic.

Cassiel

ESOTERIC AND MAGICAL SYMBOLS

The word 'magic' is derived from the Old Persian word *magus* used to describe a Zoroastrian priest of a certain rank. The Greeks used this root for their words *magikos* (magical) and *magike techne* (magical arts or the art of the Magi, the priests of the ancient world of Mesopotamia).

Magical practices were in existence in ancient Egypt, Mesopotamia and Persia, with access to its knowledge and rituals granted only to those initiated into its mysteries. Over the centuries, this restricted access led to the development of esoteric groups, who similarly restricted the mysteries to those who went through demanding rites of passage. Magical and esoteric symbols were understood by those who passed the tests, while to outsiders these symbols remained mysterious and, in many cases, frightening.

Knowledge of symbols gives us access to magical and esoteric knowledge which is still in use today. Alchemy, astrology, ceremonial magic and witchcraft all have their own sets of esoteric symbols.

Alchemy

Alchemy, which was a precursor to our modern science of chemistry, originated in the esoteric traditions of ancient Greece and Persia, although it was also practised in India and China. It dates to the 1st century CE. Knowledge of the Arabic alchemical process was recorded in *The Book of the Composition of Alchemy*, which was translated into Latin in the 12th century, widening the knowledge of alchemy in Europe. Alchemy works on three levels, the physical, the psychological and the spiritual. The first alchemists were workers in metal who produced expensive metals for the nobility.

SPIRITUAL ENLIGHTENMENT

Clouded in secrecy and believed to be concerned only with turning base metals into gold, alchemy was really concerned with the search for spiritual enlightenment. Alchemy is a spiritual quest; Carl Jung likened it to the process of psychoanalysis in which the individual explores the dark material of the unconscious in order to transform the conscious mind, achieve spiritual insight and discover the Self.

Alchemists used symbolism to disguise what the Church deemed their heretical pursuits. In Medieval and Renaissance manuscripts, which contained illustrations of alchemical processes, symbols were used to represent important components. These symbols were usually glyphs, graphic representations of a metal or instrument. Some instrument glyphs have been lost over time so, in this chapter, a drawing of the instrument is shown in its place.

THE GREAT WORK

Gold is the symbol of illumination and salvation and the final stage of the alchemical process known as the 'Great Work'. The four stages were represented by different colours: black, white, red and gold.

Alchemists began their Great Work with *materia prima* – matter which has to be found within the individual. This takes the symbolic form of a stone, which is pulverized and mixed with the first agent. It is then put in a 'Philosopher's Egg', a sealed container, and heated over a lengthy period of time. During this 'incubation' two principles within the *materia prima* emerge, which are called 'sulphur' (red, male, solar, hot energy) and 'mercury' (white, female, lunar, cold energy). These energies fight and produce *nigredo*, black putrefaction. That is the end of the first stage of the Great Work. The second stage involves the union of these to bring about the perfection of the Philosopher's Stone, the key to enlightenment.

The bain-marie is a double boiler used in the alchemical dissolution process.

HERMES TRISMEGISTUS

Hermes Trismegistus is a synthesis of the Egyptian god Thoth and the Greek god Hermes, both of whom were gods of writing and magic in their respective cultures.

Hermes Trismegistus was known as 'Hermes the Thrice Greatest' and was said to own the *Emerald Tablet*, the complete book of magic and alchemical writings.

He is credited with a set of writings on magic, mysticism and alchemy, the body of lost 'Hermetic' writing that gave rise to Hermetic mystical practices all over the world. The Hermetic philosophy systematized religious cult practices and gave the student the opportunity to find personal ascension from his base physical nature to the higher realms. The 'Hermetica' contained spells and initiation rites as well as descriptions of objects, colours and odours that should be used. There was a revival in the Hermetic tradition and its alchemical, astrological and magical practices during the Middle Ages and the Renaissance. Among these were detailed descriptions of how to protect objects, which is where the expression 'hermetically sealed' originated.

PHILOSOPHER'S STONE

In medieval symbolism, the Philosopher's Stone is the pre-eminent symbol of man's wholeness, and is represented by a pair of lions or a human couple riding on lions. It signifies passion that is so fierce that the pair wish to be one, completely united. Stones are frequent symbols for the Self as they are complete and unchanging. The alchemical stone symbolizes something that can never be lost or dissolved, and some compare it to the mystical experience of God within one's own soul. The Philosopher's Stone has been

described as lapis, a divine child, a dragon, a tincture and elixir of immortality, though it was not a physical stone. It was represented by the glyph shown below.

AILANTHUS

In Chinese alchemy, the ailanthus was known as the Tree of Life, Tree of Heaven or Paradise Tree. The elegance of the tree belied its ability to survive and thrive in the most adverse conditions and symbolizes the human ability to overcome adversity and reach spiritual grace.

CADUCEUS

In alchemy the double spiral of snakes around a rod forms the caduceus. It symbolizes the union of opposites which have to be reconciled in alchemy: mercury and sulphur, fixed and volatile, wet and dry or hot and cold. The opposites are also said to stand for solar and lunar forces, cosmic energy, polarity and duality. Some say the serpents are fighting and that they represent primal chaos, to which equilibrium is brought as they entwine around the staff. Essentially, their union is the conjunction of alchemical principles and their offspring is the Philosopher's Stone, represented by the golden ball with wings at the top of the caduceus.

The caduceus was the staff of Hermes, messenger of the gods, who revealed the secrets of alchemy. Its name is derived from the Greek *karykeion*, meaning 'herald's staff'

Materials Used in the Alchemical Process

Alchemists used a huge range of materials in their experiments, and each substance was represented by an alchemical symbol.

IRON   ANTIMONY   COPPER

TIN   LEAD   MERCURY

MAGNESIA   NICKEL   ZINC

STEEL

BISMUTH

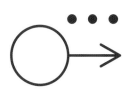

IRON FILINGS

COPPER SPLINTS

BRASS

GLASS

SULPHUR

NITRE FLOWERS

RED ARSENIC

WHITE ARSENIC

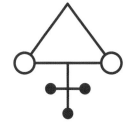

ARSENIC-SULPHUR

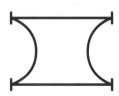

YELLOW SULPHUR

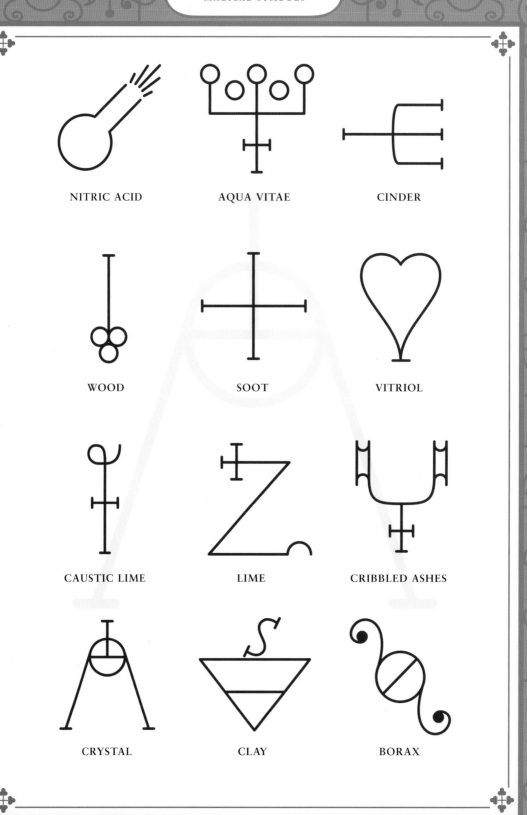

NITRIC ACID

AQUA VITAE

CINDER

WOOD

SOOT

VITRIOL

CAUSTIC LIME

LIME

CRIBBLED ASHES

CRYSTAL

CLAY

BORAX

ALUM

SOAPSTONE

BURNED PEBBLES

GRAVEL

BURNED ALUM

CHALC

STONE

POTASH

NITRE OIL

VINEGAR

BURNED HARTSHORN

URINE

VERDIGRIS

GINGER

MANURE

EGGSHELLS

SUGAR

WINE SPIRIT

YELLOW WAX

HONEY

ROCK SALT

SEA SALT

CINNABAR

Processes

The alchemical process involves solution, evaporation, precipitation and distillation.

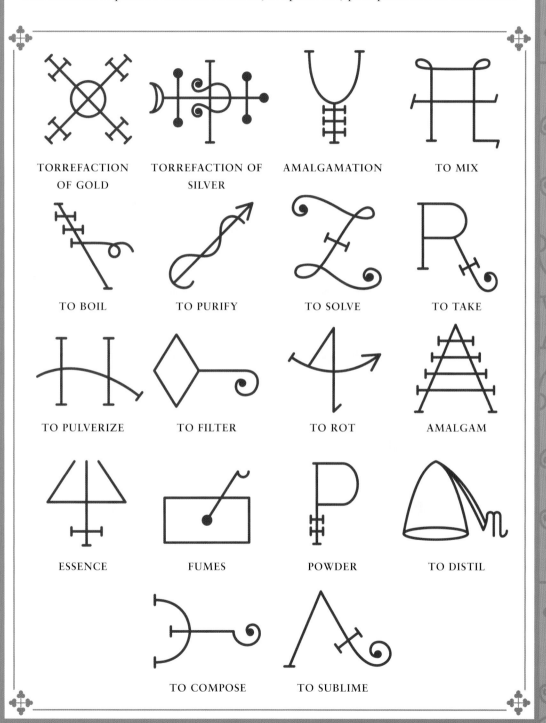

TORREFACTION OF GOLD

TORREFACTION OF SILVER

AMALGAMATION

TO MIX

TO BOIL

TO PURIFY

TO SOLVE

TO TAKE

TO PULVERIZE

TO FILTER

TO ROT

AMALGAM

ESSENCE

FUMES

POWDER

TO DISTIL

TO COMPOSE

TO SUBLIME

Instruments

The alchemists used very specific materials, instruments and procedures to achieve their transformations. Various substances went through a series of processes during which more purified, 'higher' materials were created. These processes were recorded in symbolic form to guard their secret.

ALEMBIC
The alembic is the upper part of the still used in the distillation process.

PELICAN
Named because of its resemblance to a pelican, this circulatory vessel with two side arms is used to feed condensed vapours back into its central cavity.

ALUDEL
A pear-shaped earthenware bottle, open at both ends which is used in the sublimation stage, this symbolizes the end-stage of transformation. It is also known as the Hermetic vase and the Philosopher's Egg.

ATHANOR
From the Arabic word *al-tannur* meaning 'oven', this is the furnace used to perfect matter. Shaped like a tower with a domed roof, it maintained an even temperature over long periods. Alchemists saw it as an incubator and called it 'House of the Chick'. The alchemist's furnace was used to burn away impurities.

BAIN-MARIE
The term for a warm alchemical bath, the bain-marie is a double boiler, which was used in the dissolution process. It was named after the Jewish alchemist Maria Prophetissa.

CRUCIBLE

The vessel for melting metals used by alchemists. It is usually made of porcelain so that it can withstand great heat as the metals are liquefied.

WICK

In order to maintain a constant temperature for their work, alchemists often used oil lamps with an asbestos wick, which gave a uniform warmth. They regulated the ferocity and temperature of their fire by changing the number of threads that composed the wick.

STILL

The still is used in the distillation process, whch involves heating liquid or other substances until they vaporize. The pure extract of the substance can be taken from it.

RECEIVER

The receiver is a container attached to the condensing part of the distillation apparatus. It collects the condensed products of the distillation process.

RETORT

A vessel used in the distillation process, a retort has a long, tubular neck which is bent over at the top. Substances heated over a low heat evaporate, then condense in the neck, allowing the separated liquid to be collected in an additional vessel, or receiver.

SCULL

Along with the grave and the raven, the scull symbolizes the mortification stage of the Great Work, in which blackening takes place. It represents dying to the world and transmutation, and also emphasizes the transitory nature of life.

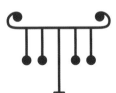

GRILLE

The grille is a metal grating or screen which provides protection from intense heat.

GLASS DROPPER

A glass dropper is used to extract and contain small amounts of liquid transferred in alchemical procedures.

Weights

Exact measurement was important in the alchemical process and standardized apothecary measures ensured that the correct weights of substances and amounts of fluids were used. Unlike the metric system, apothecary measures are based on a system including grains, minim, drams and other measures, which were assigned their individual symbols.

ONE POUND

One pound is a unit of weight equal to 454 grams or 12 ounces.

ONE OUNCE

One ounce is equal to 30 grams or 8 drams or the equivalent of 480 grains.

ONE DRAM

A dram is equal to 3.89 grams. A fluid dram is a unit of volume equal to 3.55 ml, 60 minims or 3 scruples.

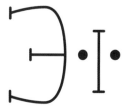

ONE SCRUPLE

A scruple is equal to 1.296 grams or 20 grains.

ONE PINCH

A pinch is the amount of a substance that can be held between the thumb and the first finger.

ONE PINT

One pint is a unit of liquid equal to 0.568 litres or 16 fluid ounces.

EQUAL QUANTITY

Alchemists were precise in their measurements and used exact equal measures in some of the processes.

Goals

The various stages of the alchemical process enabled alchemists to progress towards their goal of transforming base metals into gold or silver. Their goals also included transformation on a psychological and spiritual level, from ignorance to enlightenment.

GOLD

Judged by alchemists to be the most perfect of the metals, gold represented perfection in all matter, including in mind, body and spirit. It is associated with the coagulation stage of the Great Work and symbolizes the synthesis between the male and female principles and spiritual enlightenment, the ultimate goal of alchemists.

SILVER

One of the seven metals used in alchemy, silver is associated with distillation. It represents the unsullied nature of the *materia prima*. Silver also represents lunar or female energy and its production was associated with the goal of the first transformation stage, known as the Lesser Work.

Astrology

For many thousands of years people have watched the skies, the journey of the Sun across the heavens during the day and the stars and Moon in the night sky. In many cultures around the world people made observatories to plot these journeys and marked these sacred viewing points. The standing stones at Stonehenge in England, the pyramids in Egypt, the Inca and Maya temples in South America reflect an understanding of the movement of the celestial dome. From observation grew mythologies and knowledge about how the changing skies marked seasonal changes, which told people when to sow crops and gather in their harvest. Gradually, these were combined into the complex system we now know as astrology.

Its name originated from the Greek *astron* meaning 'star'. Ancient observers of the heavens charted the path of the Sun, Moon and stars and developed intricate systems to explain their movement through the zodiac. The glyphs depicted in this chapter come from medieval manuscripts.

HOROSCOPES

Astrologists believe that celestial events influence events on Earth and the lives of individuals and that the position of the Sun, Moon and constellations at the time of a person's birth has a profound influence on their personality and the way they lead their life. Horoscopes are a means of charting the position of the planets at the time of birth to discover what significant aspects will influence a person's life.

THE SUN SIGN

The sign of the zodiac under which a person is born is known as the Sun sign and is the dominant factor in determining character and personality. The Ascendant or rising sign is as important as a person's Sun sign and is the sign of the zodiac that was on the eastern horizon at the time of their birth. It determines the person's appearance and how he or she appears to others. The Sun sign is the person's true nature, which may be masked by the Ascendant sign.

The zodiac, or circle of animals, includes the 12 constellations that form the basis of astrology.

The Signs of the Zodiac

The zodiac means 'circle of animals' and refers to the 12 constellations. The 'northern' signs are Aries, Taurus, Gemini, Cancer, Leo and Virgo, the 'southern' signs are Libra, Scorpio, Sagittarius, Capricorn, Aquarius and Pisces.

ARIES

The symbol for Aries is the Ram's horns, but it is also linked with male genitalia and a strong sexual appetite.

TAURUS

The symbol for Taurus is the Bull and is concerned with steady growth and consolidation.

GEMINI

Gemini's symbol is the Twins and is concerned with relationships and change.

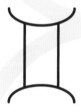

CANCER

The Crab is the symbol of Cancer and is linked with illumination and insight. The crab has a hard, protective shell into which he can retreat when the world is not as he wishes, especially where there is conflict.

LEO

Leo is represented by the lion. Leo represents controlled masculine energy, regal authority and leadership.

VIRGO

Virgo's symbol of the Virgin is associated with the flowering of crops and the fulfilment of all the hard work and tending that are required to bring projects to fruition.

LIBRA

The Scales symbolize Libra and reinforce the idea of balance because Librans love harmony and equality, weighing things up before taking action. Libra is about ideas, thoughts and the working of the mind.

SCORPIO

Scorpio is symbolized by the Scorpion or the Eagle. It is the sign most linked to interest in sex. It is also linked to death, destruction and regeneration.

SAGITTARIUS

The Archer is the symbol of Sagittarius and, like the archer, Sagittarius is involved with setting targets and reaching them.

CAPRICORN

The Goat is the symbol of Capricorn and is associated with melancholy and suffering, taking its lead from the goat that journeys up the mountain overcoming obstacles. It also symbolizes following a path of higher spiritual awareness and leaving the material world behind.

AQUARIUS

The Water Carrier is the symbol of Aquarius and unites Heaven and Earth, bringing a strong element of spirituality as the water dissolves away the old to make way for the new.

PISCES

The Fishes are the symbol of Pisces, and with the association of water, signal feminine qualities and intuition.

The Planets

Each of the planets, including the Sun and the Moon, is said to rule a Sun sign and have an influence on the way that sign manifests in an individual's life.

SUN

The Sun, considered a planet in astrology, and the centre of our solar system in astronomy, symbolizes the source of all life for many people. It also has a masculine attribute. The Sun rules the sign Leo.

MOON

The Moon, linked to the tides and menstrual cycles of women, is the only celestial body orbiting our own planet. It is often paired with the Sun and has a feminine aspect. The Moon rules the sign Cancer.

MERCURY

Mercury, named after the messenger of the gods, rules the signs Gemini and Virgo.

VENUS

Venus, named after the goddess of love, rules the signs Taurus and Libra.

MARS

Mars, named after the god of war, rules the signs Aries and Scorpio.

NEPTUNE

Neptune, named after the god of the sea, rules the sign Pisces in modern astrology.

SATURN

Saturn, named after the Roman god of agriculture, rules the signs Capricorn and Aquarius.

PLUTO

Pluto, named after the Roman god of the Underworld, rules the sign Scorpio in modern astrology.

JUPITER

Jupiter, named after the Roman god who was the equivalent of Zeus, rules the signs Sagittarius and Pisces.

URANUS

Uranus, named after the Greek god of the sky and progenitor of all the other gods, rules the sign Aquarius in modern astrology.

The Moon's Nodes

The Moon symbolizes reflection and is often connected to mirrors in which we see ourselves as we truly are. The dark side of the Moon represents the unconscious mind. The Moon's nodes are as important as the planets in Western and Vedic astrology. Sometimes called the 'dragon's head and tail', they are calculated as points on the elliptic where the Moon crosses from north to south and south to north. The dragon's head is the ascending north node and it produces positive, beneficial influences. The dragon's tail, the descending south node, is connected to negative, hindering influences. The Moon's nodes are always in direct opposition to each other.

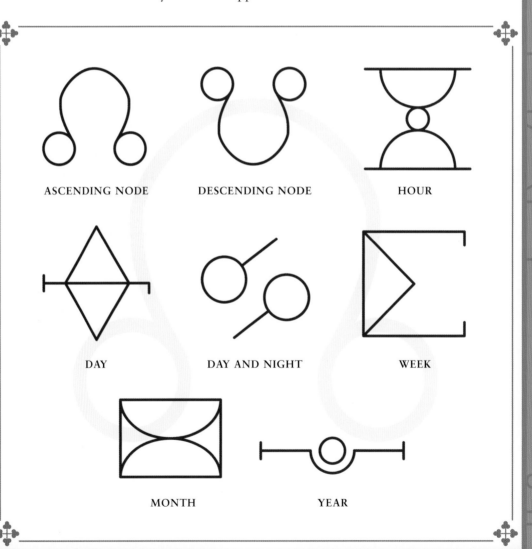

ASCENDING NODE   DESCENDING NODE   HOUR

DAY   DAY AND NIGHT   WEEK

MONTH   YEAR

Aspects

Aspects are the angles between two or more heavenly bodies that may be in the sky at the time of someone's birth; these are judged to have an influence on the individual. The aspects are divided into five major aspects and six minor aspects.

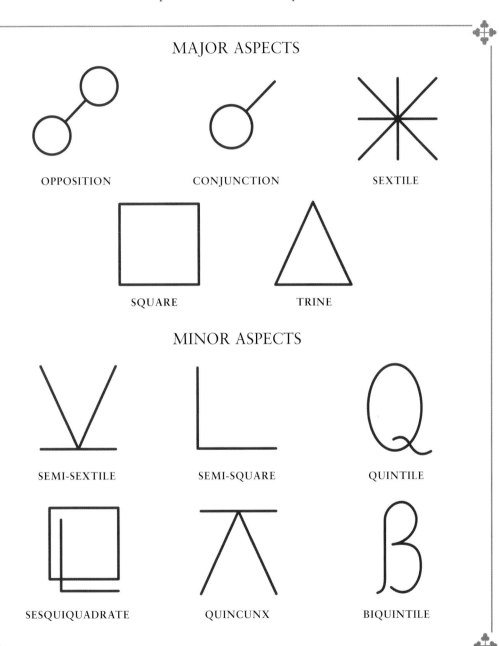

MAJOR ASPECTS

OPPOSITION   CONJUNCTION   SEXTILE

SQUARE   TRINE

MINOR ASPECTS

SEMI-SEXTILE   SEMI-SQUARE   QUINTILE

SESQUIQUADRATE   QUINCUNX   BIQUINTILE

Ceremonial Magic

Magical practices of some sort are found in almost every culture: some practices are very simple, using folk charms and herbal remedies; others are more complex, employing sophisticated ritual, incantation and ceremony. In each society, magic functions to help people influence their world. Each culture has its own rules, customs and practices, although there is some commonality, such as ritual cleansing.

AN OCCULT STUDY

The great English occultist and writer Aleister Crowley (1875–1947) defined magic as 'the science and art of causing change to occur in conformity with will'. It involves summoning the energy from a divine source in which the magician believes – the cosmos, deities or God – and using symbols and rituals to influence people or events. During the 20th century, ceremonial magic regained a certain popularity after Crowley devised his own system of ceremonial magic. He emphasized that ceremonial magic was a serious occult study and practice, and not merely a debased entertainment or stage magic.

Ceremonial magic sets out to conjure up entities to assist the magician for his own purposes. It places great emphasis on personal power or will, and involves complex rituals aimed at inducing a state of mind within the magician to allow the magic to take place, and to protect him from the wrath of the conjured entity. Prior to a magical ceremony the magician will purify himself by bathing, then dress in ceremonial robes.

MAGIC RITUAL

Like shamanistic magic, ceremonial magic is highly ritualistic and includes the use of magical objects such as knives or *athames*, swords, wooden wands, chalices, candles, salt, containers to hold incense, wine, water or herbs, drawing instruments to make magical symbols and chalk to mark out the circle in which the ritual takes place. Amulets and talismans are worn as protection, some of which have 'Words of Power' inscribed on them. Others have signs, symbols, shapes and magical squares. Occultists believe that once a symbol is created, it contains that power independent of the magician.

Some practitioners of ceremonial magic follow rituals outlined in a *grimoire*, Old French for 'grammar', a medieval book containing spells, rituals and incantations; or they may make their own 'Book of Shadows', a personal collection of ceremonies and spells. On the death of a witch this book is destroyed.

The Magic Circle is drawn to protect the magician during rituals to conjure up spirits.

The Magical Seals of the Seven Angels
of the Seven Days of the Week

In the late Middle Ages magicians practised the conjuring of spirits who would then perform their bidding. Rituals were carried out within magic circles to protect the magician from the wrath of a spirit. Some clothing and tools bore 'Words of Power', the names of the angels and archangels, which were called 'seals'. These were secret signs known only to the magician. The relevant seal would be used on the day that the ritual was performed.

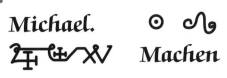

MICHAEL (SUNDAY)

GABRIEL (MONDAY)

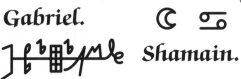

SAMAEL (TUESDAY)

RAPHAEL (WEDNESDAY)

SACHIEL (THURSDAY)

ANAEL (FRIDAY)

CASSIEL (SATURDAY)

Ceremonial Markings

During magic ceremonies the magician would wear special clothing and use tools such as wands and knives marked with protective signs and symbols. Each item of clothing and each tool would have its own seals.

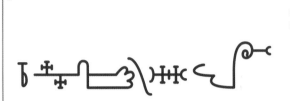

**SYMBOLS FOR MARKING
THE MAGICIAN'S ROBES**

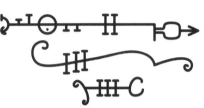

**SYMBOLS FOR MARKING
THE ASSISTANTS' GARMENTS**

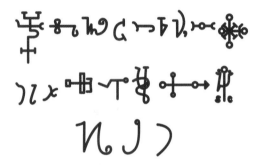

**SYMBOLS FOR MARKING
THE ASSISTANTS' CROWNS**

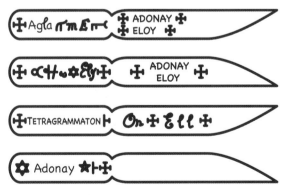

SYMBOLS FOR MARKING THE SWORD

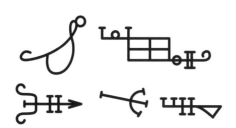

SYMBOLS FOR MARKING THE SHOES

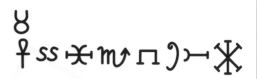

SYMBOLS FOR MARKING THE KNIFE
WITH A WHITE HILT

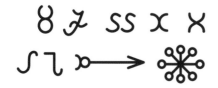

SYMBOLS FOR MARKING THE KNIFE
WITH A BLACK HILT

SYMBOLS FOR MARKING THE SCIMITAR

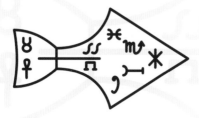

SYMBOLS FOR MARKING
THE SHORT LANCE

SYMBOLS FOR MARKING
THE DAGGER AND PONIARD

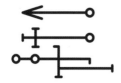

SYMBOLS FOR MARKING THE BURIN

SYMBOLS FOR MARKING THE BELL

SYMBOLS FOR MARKING THE WAND AND STAFF

SYMBOLS FOR MARKING THE TRUMPET

SYMBOLS FOR MARKING
THE SILKEN CLOTH

SYMBOLS FOR MARKING
THE VIRGIN PARCHMENT

✠ TETRAGRAMMATON ✠ JEHOVA ✠

SYMBOLS FOR MARKING THE NECROMANTIC TRIDENT

SYMBOLS FOR MARKING THE BATON

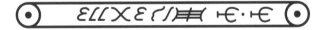

SYMBOLS FOR MARKING THE BAGUETTE

SYMBOLS FOR MARKING A MAGIC CANDLE

Signs and Seals of Demons and Spirits

In order to conjure up demons and spirits, it was necessary to know the signs and seals for particular individuals, depending on what the magician was trying to accomplish.

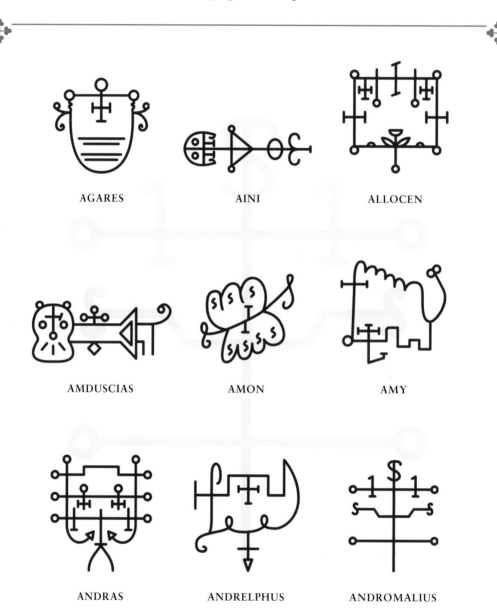

AGARES   AINI   ALLOCEN

AMDUSCIAS   AMON   AMY

ANDRAS   ANDRELPHUS   ANDROMALIUS

ASMODAY

ASTAROTH

BAAL

BALAM

BARBATOS

BATHIN

BELETH

BELIAL

BERITH

BIFRONS

BOTIS

BUER

BUNE

CAIM

CIMERIES

DANTALIAN

DECARABIA

ELIGOR

FLAUROS

FOCALOR

FORAS

FORNEUS

FURCAS

FURFUR

GAAP

GAMGYN

GLASYALABOLAS

GOMORY

GUSION

HAGENTI

HAPAS

LEAJIE

MALPAS

MARCHOSIAS

MORAX

MURMUR

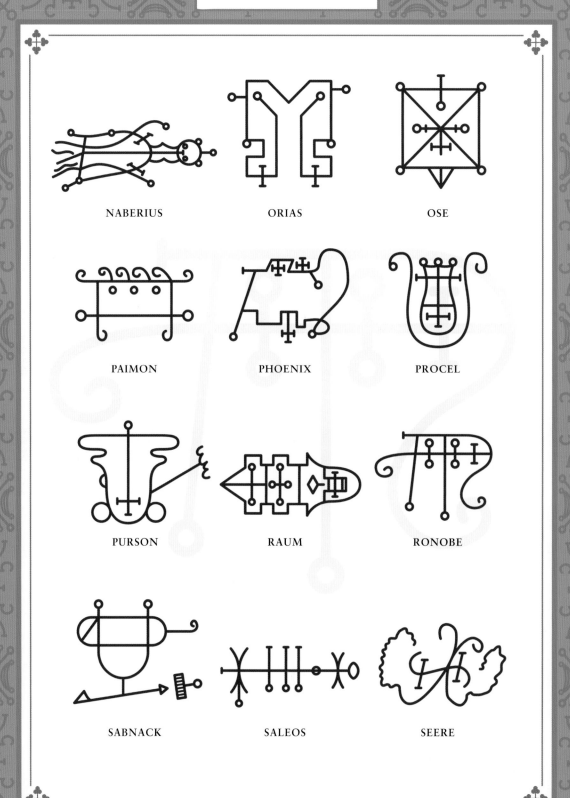

NABERIUS

ORIAS

OSE

PAIMON

PHOENIX

PROCEL

PURSON

RAUM

RONOBE

SABNACK

SALEOS

SEERE

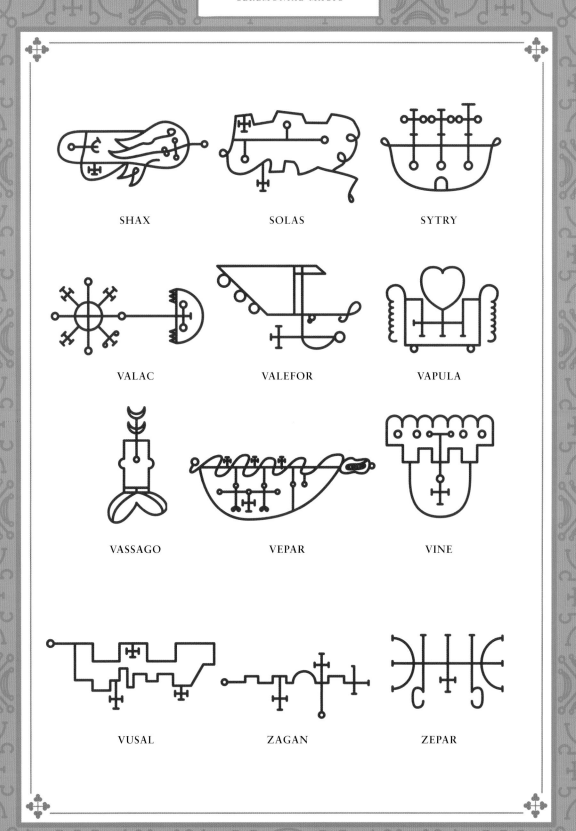

SHAX   SOLAS   SYTRY

VALAC   VALEFOR   VAPULA

VASSAGO   VEPAR   VINE

VUSAL   ZAGAN   ZEPAR

Seals of the Planets

A magical seal is a motif produced by drawing a magic number square of a planet, then connecting the numbers by a group of lines. It is also known as *kamea*.

SEAL OF THE SUN

SEAL OF THE MOON

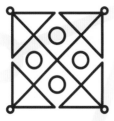

SEAL OF MERCURY

SEAL OF VENUS

SEAL OF MARS

SEAL OF JUPITER

SEAL OF SATURN

Characters of Good Spirits

Characters of good spirits bring benevolent forces to witchcraft ceremonies. They are invoked to bring positive power to aid the magical process. They include spirits from the natural world as well as guardian spirits.

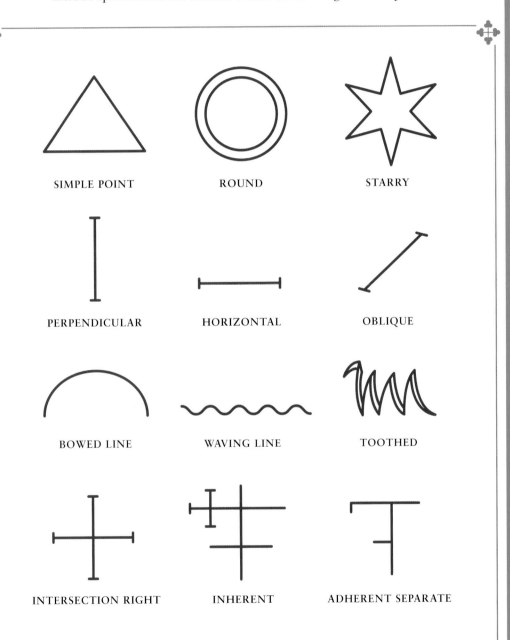

SIMPLE POINT   ROUND   STARRY

PERPENDICULAR   HORIZONTAL   OBLIQUE

BOWED LINE   WAVING LINE   TOOTHED

INTERSECTION RIGHT   INHERENT   ADHERENT SEPARATE

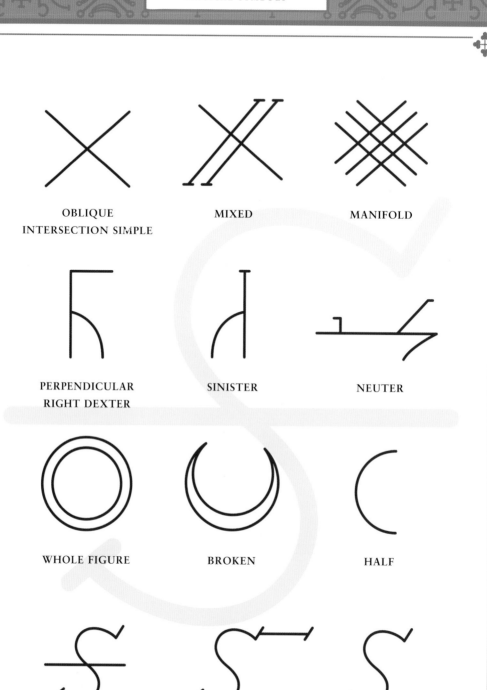

OBLIQUE
INTERSECTION SIMPLE

MIXED

MANIFOLD

PERPENDICULAR
RIGHT DEXTER

SINISTER

NEUTER

WHOLE FIGURE

BROKEN

HALF

A LETTER INHERING

A LETTER ADHERING

SEPARATE LETTER

Characters of Evil Spirits

Evil or malevolent spirits bring destructive energy to magical rituals. For this reason, witches wear pentacles to ward them off. They also inscribe their magical instruments with protective words and symbols.

RIGHT LINE	CROOKED	REFLEXED
A SIMPLE FIGURE	PENETRATE	BROKEN
A RIGHT LETTER	RETROGRADE	INVERSED
FLAME	WIND	WATER

FLYING THING

CREEPING THING

SERPENT

EYE

HAND

FOOT

CROWN

CREST

HORNS

SCEPTRE

SWORD

SCOURGE

The Magic Seals of the Three Princes of the World of Spirits

These seals symbolize inner planes of energy. Dating back to an early *grimoire*, their full significance has still to be uncovered.

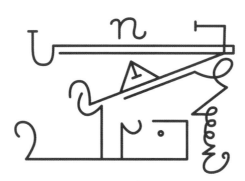

PRINCE ALMISHAK

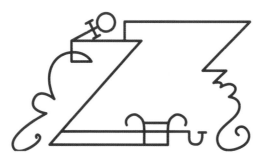

PRINCE AMABOSAR

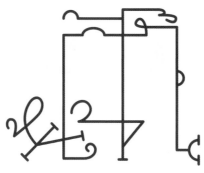

PRINCE ASHIRIKAS

Magical Alphabets

As astronomy and astrology developed, a system of secret codes or alphabets was devised in order to record the knowledge. Competition between magicians gave rise to different coded alphabets, such as Angelic, Enochian, Ogham and Theban.

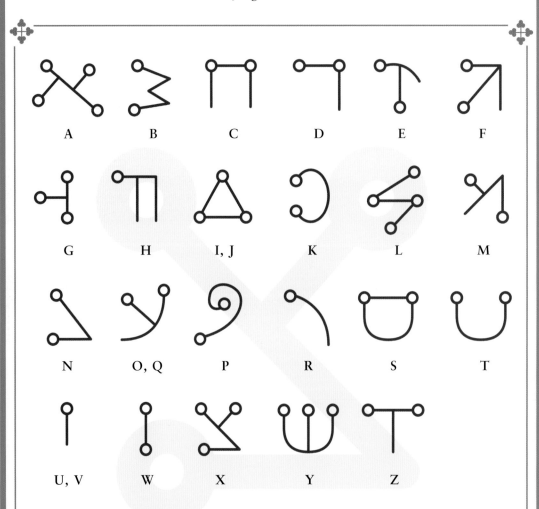

ANGELIC ALPHABET

Also known as the Celestial alphabet, the Angelic alphabet is derived from Greek and Hebrew alphabets and was created in the 16th century by Heinrich Cornelius Agrippa. It was used for communication with angels.

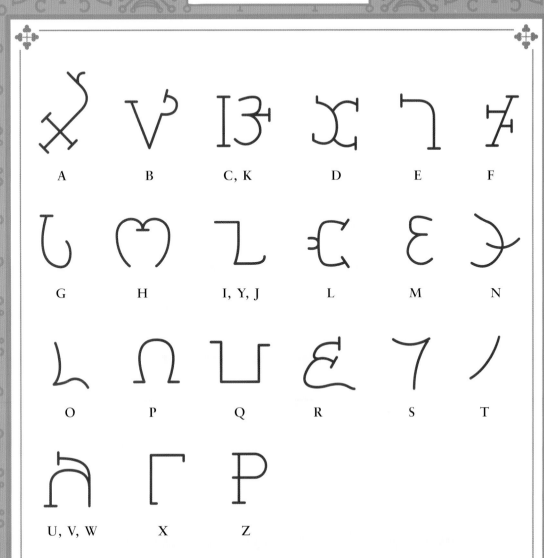

A B C, K D E F

G H I, Y, J L M N

O P Q R S T

U, V, W X Z

ENOCHIAN ALPHABET

Dr John Dee, magician and court astrologer to Queen Elizabeth I of England, and his colleague, Sir Edward Kelly, devised this alphabet in the 16th century. They said that the alphabet and the Enochian language were given to them by angels. It is used in Enochian magic or Enochian keys, which are involved in the practice of invoking angels.

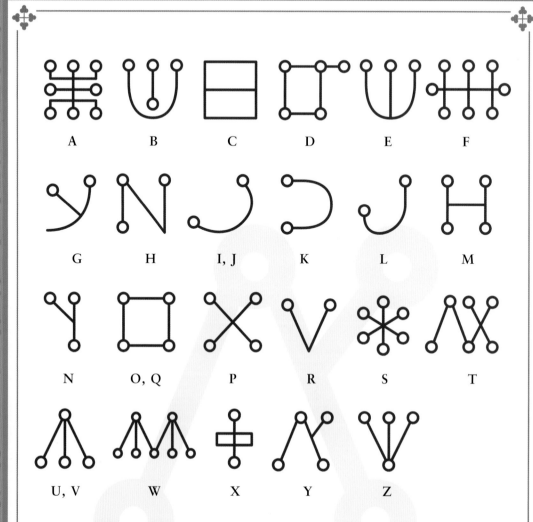

A   B   C   D   E   F

G   H   I, J   K   L   M

N   O, Q   P   R   S   T

U, V   W   X   Y   Z

MALACHIM ALPHABET

The Malachim alphabet is derived from
a combination of the Hebrew and Greek
alphabets and was created in the 16th century
by Heinrich Cornelius Agrippa. He was one
of the most influential Renaissance writers on
esoteric magic. The alphabet is still
occasionally used by the Freemasons.

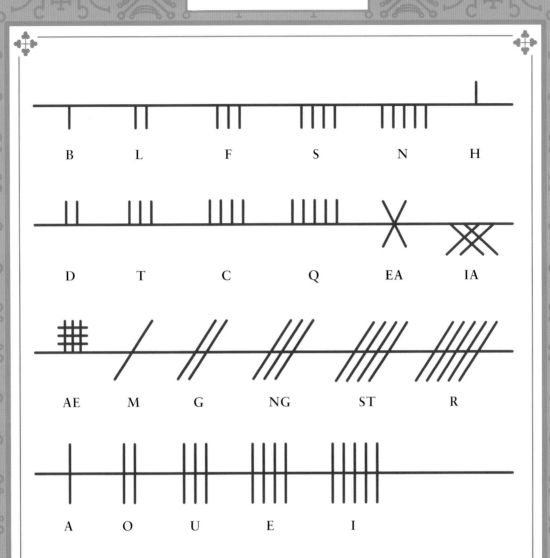

OGHAM ALPHABET

Believed to be named after the Irish god
Ogma, characters from the Ogham alphabet
have been found in Britain and Ireland since the
4th century CE. Each letter, which represents
branches or twigs, is named after a tree or
plant, and letters are linked by a line that
represents the trunk of a tree. The Eite, or
feather, is used to indicate the beginning
of a sentence and the Eite thumbnail, or
reversed feather, indicates the completion
of the sentence.

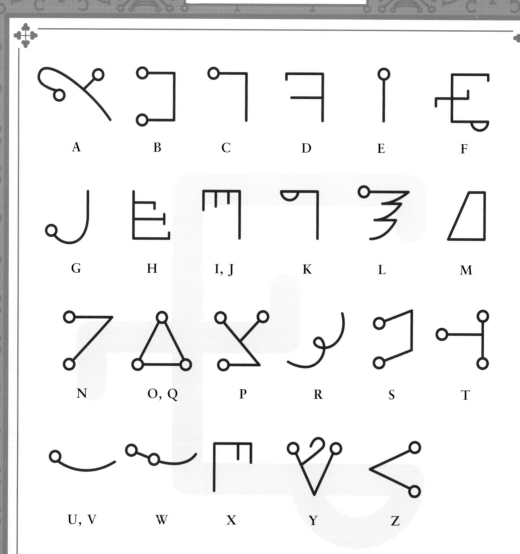

PASSING THE RIVER ALPHABET

Also known as *Passage du Fleuve*, the Passing the River alphabet was created by Heinrich Cornelius Agrippa in the 16th century and derived from the Hebrew alphabet. It is thought the name may refer to the crossing of the Euphrates by the Jews when they returned from Babylon to rebuild the Temple. The alphabet is mainly used by High Magicians.

A B C D E F

G H I, J K L M

N O P Q R S

T U, V W X Y Z

END

THEBAN ALPHABET

Although not a runic alphabet, the Theban alphabet is often called the 'Runes of Honorius' after its probable inventor Honorius of Thebes. It is utilized by witches to write spells and inscribe objects used in magic, such as talismans and amulets made of wood and stone. Also known as the 'Witch's alphabet', it is used to encode their writing to keep the meaning secret from the uninitiated. Its origins are unknown, but it was first published in Heinrich Cornelius Agrippa's *Libri Tres de Occulta Philosophia* (*Three Books of Occult Philosophy*) in 1531.

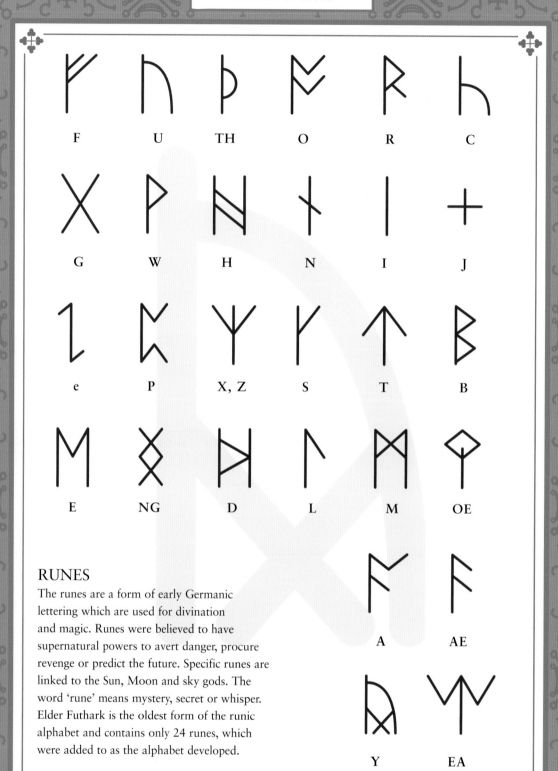

F U TH O R C

G W H N I J

e P X, Z S T B

E NG D L M OE

A AE

Y EA

RUNES

The runes are a form of early Germanic
lettering which are used for divination
and magic. Runes were believed to have
supernatural powers to avert danger, procure
revenge or predict the future. Specific runes are
linked to the Sun, Moon and sky gods. The
word 'rune' means mystery, secret or whisper.
Elder Futhark is the oldest form of the runic
alphabet and contains only 24 runes, which
were added to as the alphabet developed.

Magic Squares

Magic squares are believed to enclose or trap the potential of a power by surrounding it with a collection of numbers in a particular relationship. The simplest magic square, or *wafk*, is nine squares enclosed in a larger square in which the sum of each vertical or horizontal line adds up to nine. First made about 826, it was known as the Seal of Ghazali and used as a charm. It was written on cloth and placed beneath the feet of women in labour to ease the birth.

Some magic squares include symbols of planets, metals or magic words. The numerals and letters that made up the name of God are believed to be particularly powerful. One magic square gives the Latin sentence *Sator arepo tenet opera rotas*, which translates as 'the sower at his plough controls the work'. This has been interpreted differently by alchemists and students of the occult, but the word Latin *tenet*, 'hold', crosses the central axis and is interpreted as meaning that the cross holds up the world.

In magical squares where the numbers always add up to the same number in all the horizontal and vertical lines, the result is called the constant. Cornelius Agrippa (1486–1535) devised seven magic squares based on the seven planets: Saturn, Jupiter, Mars, the Sun, Venus, Mercury and the Moon and related metals. His book *Occulta Philosophia* describes them in detail and his magical squares are regularly used in ceremonial magic.

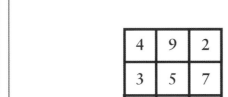

SQUARE OF SATURN   SQUARE OF JUPITER

11	24	7	20	3
4	12	25	8	16
17	5	13	21	9
10	18	1	14	22
23	6	19	2	15

SQUARE OF MARS

6	32	3	34	35	1
7	11	27	28	8	30
19	14	16	15	23	24
18	20	22	21	17	13
25	29	10	9	26	12
36	5	33	4	2	31

SQUARE OF THE SUN

22	47	16	41	10	35	4
5	23	48	17	42	11	29
30	6	24	49	18	36	12
13	31	7	25	43	19	37
38	14	32	1	26	44	20
21	39	8	33	2	27	45
46	15	40	9	34	3	28

SQUARE OF VENUS

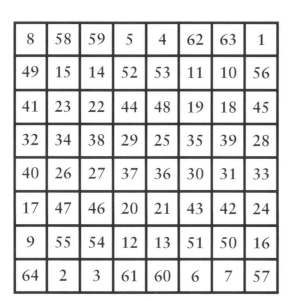

8	58	59	5	4	62	63	1
49	15	14	52	53	11	10	56
41	23	22	44	48	19	18	45
32	34	38	29	25	35	39	28
40	26	27	37	36	30	31	33
17	47	46	20	21	43	42	24
9	55	54	12	13	51	50	16
64	2	3	61	60	6	7	57

SQUARE OF MERCURY

S	A	T	O	R
A	R	E	P	O
T	E	N	E	T
O	P	E	R	A
R	O	T	A	S

SQUARE: *SATOR AREPO TENET OPERA ROTAS*

37	78	29	70	21	62	13	54	5
6	38	79	30	71	22	63	14	46
47	7	39	80	31	72	23	55	15
16	48	8	40	81	32	64	24	56
57	17	49	9	41	73	33	65	25
26	58	18	50	1	42	74	34	66
67	27	59	10	51	2	43	75	35
36	68	19	60	11	52	3	44	76
77	28	69	20	61	12	53	4	45

SQUARE OF THE MOON

Witchcraft

Witchcraft is the practice of using supernatural forces or magical powers and is concerned with sorcery and divination. 'Witch' comes from Old English *wicca*, pronounced *whitcha*, meaning a male witch, and *wicce*, pronounced *witcheh*, a female witch. *Wiccan* means to cast a spell. It takes different forms according to the country or tradition in which it is practised. Powers ascribed to witches include the ability to fly, particularly on a broomstick, to change shape and form, to cast spells, curse and harm people or to protect them.

PRACTICES

Some form of witchcraft exists in almost every society and is based on the concept that the cosmos is whole and interconnected at every level. The witch brings his or her knowledge of magical rites and incantations to influence these connections to bring about change. In using ritual magic, wizards seek to communicate with the unseen forces that shape our lives and control the forces of nature. The aim of witchcraft is to influence another person or their property, to gain wealth, health or personal power. In *Malefic* or black magic, the aim is to bring unwanted misfortune to others. Such dark practices were thought to cause death, bad luck, disease in animals and other misfortunes.

White magic is used to counteract black magic or to bring about good fortune, to help barren women conceive or bring well-being. White witchcraft is the term for beneficent magical practice.

From the Greek *nekros* meaning 'dead' and *manteia*, meaning 'divination', necromancy is a form of divination. The witch summons the spirit of the dead person or 'conjures' him to appear in the room in which the conjuring is taking place. Their spirit is brought into the present to provide information about future events.

With the growing power of Christianity, old magical practices were driven underground and witches practised in secret. Wherever there are secret groups, brotherhoods and esoteric societies they are feared and distrusted by those on the outside. Witches and wizards have been lauded and reviled at different points in history. Some religions regard all forms of witchcraft as the work of the devil and condemn it and the practitioners of the 'dark arts'. They associated it with heresy, and used their powers to persecute and kill witches, a common occurrence throughout Europe during the Middle Ages and even later.

WICCA

Wiccans and Neo-pagans, who use ritual as part of their beliefs, have been responsible for a positive exploration of witchcraft in modern times. The belief is held in contemporary witchcraft that power of witchcraft comes from psychological and psychosomatic effects rather than paranormal intervention.

Modern Wiccan Rede. or law, forbids the hurting of others.

The Neo-pagan Wiccan tradition holds with the 'Threefold Law of Return', which states that whatever the witch does to others magically will come back threefold. Modern white witches believe it is unethical to direct magic towards anyone

The Book of Shadows *contains a witch's personal collection of spells and is destroyed on her death.*

who has not consented to it. Wicca emphasizes the benefits of making up personal spells. Other folk-magic practitioners prefer to use spells handed down from the elders.

WITCH'S PENTANGLE

The pentangle is a symbol of witchcraft and is a five-pointed star with four points representing the four directions while the fifth point symbolizes the sanctity of spirit; the circle round it represents the quest for divine knowledge. As with other figures made of a single unbroken line, it represents a continuous connection to cosmic forces. The pentangle within a circle is used to mark off magical enclosures or ritual areas, especially when used to invoke spirits or practise magical ceremonies. Some Satanic rites invert the pentangle to summon demonic spirits.

The pentangle is widely used in Wicca and ceremonial magic and when the image of the pentangle is drawn, it is known as a pentagram. In working magic the pentangle is drawn in the air with the athame, or sacred blade. A physical pentangle in the form of a flat disc is placed on the altar; the symbol is also used as decoration on magical tools such as chalices or on the handle of the athame. The pentangle is worn by Neo-pagans in the form of rings and pendants for protection and to indicate they are involved in the world of magic.

The Pythagoreans considered this widespread sacred sign to be the symbol of life and the divine human. Followers of Pythagoras called it the *Pentalpha* as it is composed of five interlaced As or Alphas (Alpha being the first letter of the Greek alphabet). When the Pythagoreans were persecuted, it became the secret symbol of the followers, 'so they would know each other'.

Degrees

In Wicca or other forms of witchcraft there is a system of initiation known as the degree system. This system marks the progress of the new candidate through a series of ceremonies as their level of understanding and proficiency in the craft advance. Wicca, the Craft of the Wise, has three degrees. Symbols representing the different degrees are drawn after the witch's Wiccan name to indicate the level of their rank or position. They also represent the salutes given at the different levels as the hand touches various parts of the body in a single, uninterrupted motion.

FIRST DEGREE

The First Degree is open to all who want to enter the path of witchcraft and inducts the witch into the coven. It introduces them to the basic teachings and traditions. The inverted triangle represents the points in the 'Threefold salute' of the First Degree: breast, breast, genitals and return to breast. In some practices this is reversed.

SECOND DEGREE (I)

The Second Degree marks progress to the deeper knowledge of witchcraft and the sustained commitment to the craft law and practice. The first level of the symbol is the triangle with the point at the top. The 'Threefold Salute' follows the triangle in the pattern of mouth, breast, breast, mouth. The triangle in this position also symbolizes fire.

SECOND DEGREE (II)

The Fivefold Salute of the Second Degree follows the shape of the pentagram: genitals, right breast, left hip, right hip, left breast, genitals. The 'Star of Knowledge' is the name given by the Roma people to the pentagram revealed when an apple is cut across, which connects the symbol to the Tree of Knowledge.

THIRD DEGREE

The Third Degree is granted to witches who have shown a high level of proficiency or to Elders of the coven. It represents the salute of mouth, breast, breast, mouth, genitals, right foot, left knee, right knee, left foot, genitals. Once this level has been bestowed it enables those who have attained this level to form their own covens.

The Book of Shadows

After a witch is initiated into a coven, she builds a personal collection of
spells, rituals, recipes for herbal preparations and anything else that helps
her perform magic. Some include details of the properties of herbs, such
as 'the Banefuls', including belladonna or deadly nightshade (a source of
the drug atropine, which in small quantities eases pain, but in stronger
doses can kill). *The Book of Shadows* will usually include information
about the best time to cast spells and the meaning of a number of symbols
is also included. The *Book of Shadows* is kept secret and is traditionally
destroyed when the witch dies.

EARTH

AIR

FIRE

WATER

Hexes

'Hex' comes from 19th-century Pennsylvanian German *Hexencraft*, which means witchcraft. It is mainly used as a curse to bring misfortune, though others believe hexes can be used in beneficial spell-making, such as animal fertility spells or home protection spells. The Pennsylvanian group designed a series of hex signs which they painted on their barn doors to bring good fortune.

TRIPLE STAR

LUCKY STARS

OAK LEAVES AND ACORNS

SYMBOLS FROM THE NATURAL WORLD

The relationship between the natural world of trees, plants and the elements has always been crucial to the survival of the human race. Earliest civilizations believed that spirits living in trees and rocks needed to be venerated in case they turned against humans who had so little control over their environment.

The early Romans decorated their dwelling places with evergreens as a way of showing hospitality to the spirits who haunted their woods; today, trees are still invested with magical powers. Some are decorated with messages attached by ribbons that ask for the intervention of the particular deity or spirit that the tree represents. In France in an isolated place with no tourist signs to direct people to it, a tree dedicated to the magician Merlin is festooned with coloured bows and with requests for help and notes of thanks for previous successful intervention. The belief in the mystical power of trees and plants is held throughout the world.

Our early ancestors recognized the solstices, the shortest and longest days, and marked them by carrying out rituals and celebrations. The winter solstice was celebrated in pagan Scandinavia with the Yule festival, the early Celts hung mistletoe over doorways as a sign of goodwill to visitors and the Inca held midwinter ceremonies at temples used as astronomical observatories.

The symbolism of plants is often based on the theory of correspondences. The Doctrine of Signatures holds that everything in nature is marked with a pattern or 'signature' that reveals its innate properties.

Trees and Plants

The tree is one of the most widely recognized symbols of humanity. The long, vertical shape of the tree symbolizes the centre of the world that links the Underworld, the Earth and the Heavens. From ancient times trees were connected to gods and mystical forces in nature, with fertility, spirits and divine energy. The Tree of Life or World Tree was said to span Heaven and Earth. Mythological connections between gods and trees are widespread: the Egyptian god Osiris is linked with the cedar and the Greek god Apollo with the laurel.

TREE WORSHIP

Trees are important symbols in Celtic tradition. They provide the link between Earth and Heaven, the upper and lower worlds and the eternal life after death; as such they were venerated. At the Saturnalia festival the Romans decorated trees with candles and on 1 January they brought larch boughs into their homes to symbolically 'bring in' the New Year.

Tree worship was found in all places where trees grew. The evergreen symbolizes long life. Deciduous trees were the centre of pagan Earth Mother fertility rites. With their stripped branches in winter and the return of spring growth, they symbolized death and regeneration. In some areas of the Mediterranean and in India, women who want to conceive tie red handkerchiefs or strips of red cloth to the lower branches of lone trees growing beside a spring.

Different cultures ascribe different attributes to trees, though the ever-present cosmic connection is a thread that weaves together differing perceptions of tree symbolism. In Scandinavia, the sacred tree was the ash or cosmic ash, also known as *Yggdrasil*, which grew between Asgard, the home of the gods, Midgard, the place of humans, and Hel, the Underworld and is the symbol of universal life. It had three roots, one in the god-world, one in the material world and the third in *Niflheim*, the cloud-world. The Maya believed that branches of the sacred tree *Yaxche* held up the heavens.

According to some legends, when Adam left the Garden of Eden he took a sprig from the Tree of Knowledge. From this he grew a tree which provided the wood that was made into the cross on which Jesus Christ was crucified.

Forests symbolize places of transformation, where magical ceremonies were performed in secret. Entering the forest symbolized the entrance to an unknown place, the darkness, where man could experience mystical events and learn concealed truths. To come out into the light as a changed person symbolized the exploration of the unconscious mind and becoming 'enlightened'.

The olive tree was sacred to the Greek goddess Athena and its leaves were made into crowns for victors of the Olympic games.

APPLE TREE

In Christian and Jewish texts the apple is the symbol of original sin since God warned Adam and Eve not to eat the apple from the Tree of the Knowledge of Good and Evil. When they ate the forbidden fruit they were expelled from the Garden of Eden and fell from grace. *Malus* is the Latin for 'apple' and for 'evil'. The apple as a symbol of discord is echoed in the Greek story of the golden apple. Paris was to give the apple to the fairest goddess and chose Aphrodite, which so enraged other goddesses that it led to the Trojan War. It symbolizes earthly desires and indulgence.

Apples feature in magic rituals and are linked to goddess worship. It was believed that if you wrote a holy name on an apple and ate it over three consecutive days it would cure a fever.

OAK

Sacred to the god Zeus (Jupiter), the oak represents strength, steadfastness and endurance. At the ancient shrine of Dodona, dedicated to Zeus, priests interpreted the rustling of the oak trees as messages from Zeus. One myth says that Jason's ship, the *Argo*, was built of oak from Dodona, and that one of the beams spoke and gave advice to Jason's men, the Argonauts, as they sailed in search of the Golden Fleece. In Rome crowns of oak leaves were given to victorious generals.

The oak was venerated by the Celts, who gathered in sacred oak groves and performed their magic rituals. Druids gathered mistletoe from its branches for use in fertility rites. In pre-Christian times it was the Tree of Life. The oak, its leaves and the acorn stand for strength, leadership and success in battle.

OLIVE TREE

The olive was sacred to the goddess Athena and a wreath of wild olive branches was given to the victor of the Olympic games. The doors and posts of Solomon's temple were made of olive wood, and olive oil was used in the consecration of Jewish priests. The olive branch is associated with the dove and both the branch and the dove symbolize peace.

LAUREL (BAY)

In Rome, laurel was the emblem of Apollo and was associated with glory, victory and reward. Romans believed that a laurel wreath protected the wearer from lightning, and Julius Caeser was always depicted wearing one, though it also symbolized the crown of the victor. Roman priests used laurel twigs to sprinkle water or sacrificial blood in temple ceremonies, which may have been the origin of sprinkling Holy Water in Christian services.

The Greeks gave a wreath made of laurel to the winner of the games at Delphi. The ancient Greeks believed that laurel gave the gift of prophecy and poetry; priestesses of the Python were crowned with laurel and it was placed under pillows to bring inspiration. In China it was associated with victory and eloquence.

HAZEL

Believed to have magical powers, especially in water divination, hazel is associated with mysterious attributes, probably because its deep roots were believed to tap into the Underworld. In the Celtic world it was used to make magicians' wands and the wood became known as 'witch-hazel'. It was believed that hazel rods could discover treasure as well as water. The rod of Hermes, the messenger of the gods, was made of hazel.

Hazel was sacred to the god Thor and at one time it was customary for captains of European ships to wear a cap woven with hazel twigs as a talisman against rough seas. They believed it could save the ship from the worst storms and keep the sailors safe. It is also associated with fertility and was used as a charm to bring luck to lovers.

PALM

In ancient Rome, the palm was the symbol of Osiris. It signified his union with Isis, and the palm tree represented his erect penis when he was reincarnated as Menu, the Bull. The palm tree had a similar phallic symbolism in the Phoenician cult of Baal-Peor, where worship included sensuous indulgence. In Rome the palm was bestowed on victorious gladiators. It is also the symbol of spiritual victory.

The branches of the palm tree are carried at the feast of Tabernacles, and when Jesus entered Jerusalem, crowds greeted him with palm fronds. It is a symbol of Christ's victory over death and is associated with Easter when palm leaves are given to worshippers after church services. Palm leaves were used in funeral rituals as they symbolized the afterlife.

The ancient Hebrews decorated their coins with palms as they grew plentifully in Palestine, and later it became the symbol of Israel. It is said that the palm tree grows faster when weighed down with its fruit, hence its symbolism as having the ability to overcome adversity by resolute determination.

PINE

As an evergreen, the pine is a symbol of survival and regeneration. The tradition of bringing a tree inside the home at the darkest point in winter, then decorating it with candles, celebrated the knowledge that the dark would pass and lightness would return in the light of spring. The present custom of hanging bright baubles and lights on Christmas trees originated at a time when there was no artificial light.

Pine cones were a sign of masculine fertility to ancient Greeks because of their erect nature and their abundance. The Assyrians used the sexual symbolism of the pine in combination with the female lotus as decoration of their temples in the style of the egg-and-dart frieze.

CEDAR

A symbol of strength and fidelity, the cedar is the emblem of Lebanon. The wood for the temple of Solomon is reputed to be cedar. Its gum was used for embalming and its wood was used in building royal palaces.

The cedar was often found near oracular shrines because it was believed to have the power to reveal the secrets of Heaven and to have magical powers that drove away evil spirits. In Sumerian mythology it is the Cosmic Tree, the Tree of Life sacred to the god Tammuz and is imbued with magical properties.

FIG TREE

The fig tree was the sacred tree of India, and along with the olive tree and the vine, it is a symbol of plenty and immortality. It represents religious wisdom and was used by ancient Egyptians in initiation rites. Later, in the biblical story when Adam and Eve realized they were without clothes, they sewed fig leaves together to cover their nakedness. Fig leaves have been used down the centuries in painting and on sculptures to cover the genitals as a symbol of modesty and chastity.

In eastern Asia a particular genus of fig, the banyan tree, is the everlasting tree of the Upanishads and is known as the World Tree that links Heaven and Earth. The banyan is the home of spirits which symbolize life and procreation. In Buddhism, as the Bodhi Tree under which the Buddha attained enlightenment, it is identified as the world's axis. The Buddha becomes one with the axis of the world. For Buddhists it symbolizes learning, immortality and enlightenment.

The opposite of the Tree of Life is the Tree of Death. When stripped bare of foliage and withered, the fig represents the opposite of life and confirms the duality of symbols. Christians thought the Tree of Death represented the failure of the synagogue to recognize Jesus as the Messiah.

SHEAF OF CORN

In England, the last sheaf of corn represents the 'spirit of the field' and parts of it were made into corn dolls. These were then drenched in water to symbolize the rain needed to ensure growth, or burned to symbolize the death of the grain spirit. The heraldic term for a sheaf of corn is *garbe* and it symbolizes the bread eaten at the Last Supper. The astrological sign Virgo, the Virgin, is often depicted with a sheaf of corn, the symbol of harvest.

BUSHEL OF WHEAT

In Christianity the grain of wheat is a symbol for Christ. It symbolizes the body of Christ and signifies resurrection through the partaking of sacramental bread and wine, which represent the body and blood of Christ. The bushel of wheat symbolizes the divine harvest.

CORNUCOPIA

Known as the 'Horn of Plenty', the cornucopia is a symbol of abundance. Originally it was associated with the Great Cow goddess in her incarnation as Ceres, Hathor and other versions of the sacred cow.

In Greek mythology, when Zeus was a baby, he was put in the care of the daughters of King Melisseus and the goat-nymph Amaltea. He was so thankful for their kindness that he broke off one of the goat's horns and gave it to them, saying that it would always be filled with food and drink. Cornucopia are used as decoration to symbolize unending plenty.

IVY

The holly, the ivy and the yew were held in great respect by the Celts because they were green all year round and were a symbol of immortality. Ivy was associated with the lunar goddess Arianhod and the journey to the Other World, the mystical dark side. It is a feminine symbol denoting a need for protection. The power of ivy is in its ability to bind and cling, making it a potent symbol of determination. It also signifies friendship, fidelity and marriage. It was customary in Victorian times for the new bride to take the ivy from her bouquet and plant it so that it could be passed on to her daughter and granddaughter for their bridal bouquets.

SHAMROCK

One of the family of three-leaved clovers, the shamrock is an ancient Celtic symbol. It became the emblem of Ireland after St Patrick used it to demonstrate the Christian concept of the Trinity. As he also drove all the snakes out of Ireland, legend has it that no snake would ever touch a shamrock.

LOTUS

The lotus or sacred water lily is a common feature in art and decoration in ancient Egypt (see page 14). It symbolizes the life-giving power of the River Nile and is associated with Osiris, Lord of the Dead. Its unfolding petals are likened to the expansion of the soul or the gradual wakening of the spirit to light.

Hindus associate the lotus blossom with the gods Vishnu, Brahma and Lakshmi. It is sacred to them because it symbolizes enlightenment and spiritual revelation and their belief that the god Brahma was born in a lotus. In Hindu and Buddhist art, gods are frequently represented sitting on lotus thrones. Hindus also associate it with divine beauty and Sri Krishna is frequently described as the 'Lotus-eyed One'.

In Buddhist symbolism the lotus represents purity of mind and action, as the flower rises above the mud which holds its roots. This is also a symbol of detachment from base human desires and worldly attachment.

VINE

For the people of Palestine and the surrounding regions, the vine was sacred and the wine it produced was the drink of the gods. The vine symbolizes youth and everlasting life. It was sacred to Dionysus (Bacchus), god of wine, and many images depict him entwined in vines. The grape represents sacrifice and fertility as it was made into the wine drunk at the Bacchanalian revels, and sacrifices were made to the god.

In Christian symbolism it represents Christ who said, 'I am the true vine' (John 15:1) and it is widely found in church decoration and signifies direct contact with Christ. Wine symbolizes the blood of Christ when it is taken at Holy Communion.

The Tree of Life is depicted as a vine and the Sumerian written sign for 'life' was usually a vine leaf.

Flowers

For thousands of years and throughout the world, flowers have been religious and national symbols, used in rituals, in celebration and in mourning. Neanderthal man made flower offerings to the dead, and ancient paintings and carvings are full of flowers and other forms of plant life. They are woven into the tapestry of life and given as tokens of love or thanks, at births, marriages and deaths. Growing from the earth and responding to the natural elements of the sun and rain, they represent the cycle of life, in which we 'flower' and then decline, only to be reborn from the fruit of the flower. In the Hindu tradition the flower is related to *ether*, the spirit.

In ancient times flowers symbolized the work of the Sun, and yellow and orange flowers intensified this connection.

The ancient Greeks developed a language of flower symbolism called *floriography* which continued over many centuries.

A garland of flowers combines the symbolism of the flowers and the ring, a symbol of eternity. It is associated with good fortune and fertility. Flowers in bouquets sent today carry specific meanings: red roses for love, white roses for purity, while arum lilies are often included in funeral wreaths as a sign of sorrow and sympathy.

IKEBANA

The Japanese have developed a highly stylized system of flower-arranging called *Ikebana*. In the complex system of floral symbols the precepts of Buddhism are invoked, where deliberate understatement, *wabi*, is used. The arrangements are in three tiers; the bottom tier represents the Earth, the middle tier humanity and the top tier represents Heaven.

In Eastern lands they talk in flowers,
And they tell in a garland their loves and
* cares;*
Each blossom that blooms in their garden
* bowers*
On its leaves a mystical language wears.

JOHN INGRAM

Flowers used in decoration, from buildings to gravestones, carry symbolic messages.

LILY

The lily is referred to frequently in the Bible and the early Jews decorated the first temple with images of lilies, which symbolized unadorned, pure beauty. In Christian symbolism, the lily represents chastity, purity and sorrow. It is said that as Eve wept when she left the Garden of Eden, lilies grew where her tears fell. In Catholic countries the lily is dedicated to the Virgin Mary as a symbol of her purity and it is also the Easter symbol of the resurrection.

The Christian 'chalice' (cup) derived from the calyx (cup) of the lily, and thus the symbol of the female container or womb is associated with this flower. In the Middle East, the lily was the sacred flower of Astarte, who was also called Lilith, from the Sumerian *lilu*, a lotus. Many see the lily as the Western equivalent of the lotus. The lily was dedicated to the goddess Juno and symbolized majesty. In Japan and China, the lily was believed to have the power to lessen grief and women in mourning wore it tucked in their belts.

ROSE

The rose is perhaps the most important flower symbolically and is mentioned in early Greek and Hebrew writing. In ancient times it was the emblem of silence as well as love, and on festive occasions a rose was suspended over the table, indicating that the conversations were *sub rosa*, secret, not to be repeated outside the gathering. The rose symbolized joy to the Romans, and Comus, the god of feasting, is depicted wearing a garland of roses.

The rose is sacred to many goddesses and the Christian Church made it sacred to the Virgin Mary. Christians associated the five petals of the rose with the five wounds of Christ. Rose windows in churches are a symbol of the Virgin and usually face west, the direction of Paradise. The Golden Rose was given to sovereigns by the pope as an emblem of the mortality of the body, and the gold from which it was made symbolized the immortality of the soul.

Roses are significant in alchemical and hermetic symbolism: the golden rose symbolizes perfection, a blue rose that which is unattainable, the seven-petalled rose represents days of the week and seven degrees of enlightenment, and the eight-petalled rose symbolizes regeneration.

FLEUR-DE-LIS

In 12th-century France, King Philip I chose the fleur-de-lis as the emblem for the country. It originated in the Gaulish symbol of the Lily Maid, a form of the god Juno, whose emblem was a lily, since she fertilized herself using a magic lily to conceive her son, the god Mars. The symbol became associated with the Virgin Mary, who also conceived without male connection.

As the lily was such a sacred symbol it was included on many coats of arms and banners. A red fleur-de-lis is the heraldic symbol of the Italian city of Florence.

TULIP

In Turkey, where the tulip originated, it was regarded as the flower of perfect love and symbolized a declaration of love. In the Ottoman Empire, the Turkish word for tulip was written using the same letters that formed the word for Allah, symbolizing purity and divinity, and later the tulip became the emblem of the Ottoman rulers.

In the Netherlands, in the 17th century, tulipmania caused tulip bulbs to be bought and sold at extraordinary prices – £5,000 in one instance. The tulip is the national symbol of the Netherlands.

POPPY

From the poppy we get opium and its offspring, morphine and heroin, so it is associated with sleep, unconsciousness and death. In ancient Greece the poppy was dedicated to Hypnos, the god of sleep, and Morpheus, the god of dreams. Demeter, the goddess of death, was frequently shown carrying poppies, as she was picking them when Hades snatched her and took her to the Underworld. However, it is also a symbol of fertility because the poppy produces so many seeds.

Red poppies have been used to commemorate fallen soldiers since the First World War because they blossomed in the shelled and bombed fields of France where so many were killed. In many countries, wreaths of red poppies are placed on war memorials on Remembrance Sunday when all soldiers who have died in war are remembered.

Herbs

In ancient civilizations people believed that herbs were first discovered by the gods and were therefore linked to celestial intervention.

Some herbs are known as apotropaic because they have the ability to guard us from evil influences or bad luck, from the Greek *apotropaios* meaning 'to avert evil'.

HERBS AS MEDICINE

The power of herbs to heal all manner of illness has been linked to the divine. The early Christians believed that medicinal herbs worked successfully because they were first found on Calvary, where Christ was crucified.

Early Celtic healers used medicinal herbs extensively and based their belief in their curative powers because of the link to the Fountains of Health, *Slante*. Herbs are both medicinal and poisonous, and carry the ability to bring health or death – because of this power they appear frequently in magic, folk stories and legends.

Animals also had a part to play in herb lore. Deer were supposed to be able to find medicinal herbs. A deer shot by an arrow, with herbs in its mouth, symbolized love sickness and related to Cupid's bow and arrow.

The Doctrine of Signatures theory uses the similarity of the herb shape to a physical part of the body; for example the trefoil with heart-shaped leaves was used to treat heart disorders.

EMOTIONAL CONNECTIONS

Shakespeare's Ophelia in *Hamlet* speaks of the meaning of the flowers and herbs she carries: rosemary for remembrance, pansies for thought and rue, herb of grace and regret. Rue was used to ward off evil spirits and priests sprinkled holy water from rue sprigs.

Thyme symbolizes purity while sage is the symbol for wisdom and immortality. *Tulsi*, or sweet basil, is known as Holy Basil.

Ophelia in Shakespeare's Hamlet *speaks of the symbolism of herbs in the famous scene after she has been rejected by Hamlet.*

BASIL

An apotropaic herb, basil was used at
funerals and in rites for the dead to prevent
any misfortune happening to the deceased.
It originated in India where sweet basil, or
tulsi, was sacred to the god Vishnu. At death,
a basil leaf was placed on the chest of the
deceased to open the gates of Heaven so
that the departed might enter.

In Elizabethan England when guests
departed they were given a small pot of basil
to ensure a safe passage home. In Italy, basil
signified love and traditionally a woman who
was ready to receive a suitor would place a
pot of basil on her balcony.

Ancient Greeks used basil as an antidote
to the fatal venom of the basilisk, a mythical
creature whose gaze could strike a person
dead on the spot.

MISTLETOE

Since antiquity mistletoe has been used as a
medicine to boost the health of those who
were run down; it has been proven to have
the ability to strengthen the immune system.
Evergreen with fruits in midwinter, a rarity
that attracted attention over the centuries,
mistletoe symbolizes growth and renewal at
the darkest times, as well as regeneration.
The yellow colour of the withered mistletoe
branch was believed, by the process of
sympathetic magic, to have the power to find
hidden gold. The 'Golden Bough' was used
in animal sacrifices.

Mistletoe was sacred to the Druids who
used it for its healing powers and as a cure
for infertility. It appears to thrive in winter
when the host tree seems dead. The Druid
priests believed the most powerful mistletoe
came from oak trees and used it as a
protection against poison. The Norse god
Balder lost his immortality when he was
pierced by a spear tipped in mistletoe.
Legend has it that the Druids cut mistletoe
from trees using golden sickles and then
wrapped it in white cloth so it would not
touch the ground; in this way they
maintained the mystical strength of the plant.
The connection with fertility lives on in the
Christmas custom of kissing under mistletoe.

LAVENDER

'Lavender' comes from the Latin *lavere* and means 'to wash'. The Romans brought it to the many parts of Europe which they conquered. Roman soldiers took lavender in their herbal 'first-aid' kit. They knew about its antiseptic and insect-repelling qualities, and in Europe it was grown by medieval monks who valued its calming properties. English lavender, *Lavandula angustifolia*, provides an essential oil which is used in skin salves and ointments. It is also used as a sleeping aid. Lavender water can be sprinkled on bed linen or a bunch of dried lavender can be placed under a pillow.

ROSEMARY

This herb symbolizes love, fidelity and remembrance. It was used at funerals and sprigs were dropped on the coffin as a sign that the deceased would not be forgotten. It is often planted in graveyards. The herbalist Nicholas Culpeper (1616–1654) believed it could be used to strengthen memory, and in ancient Greece students wore sprigs of rosemary on their clothes to enhance their memory during examinations.

The Latin name *Rosmarinus* translates as 'rose of the sea', a name given to Venus, and with that link rosemary is thought to be an aphrodisiac.

SAGE

Named after the wise woman Saga, sage is a symbol of wisdom, or sagacity. The ancient Greeks associated it with maturity and wisdom. It is used in cleansing and purification rituals by First Nations people in North America, where dried sage is tied in bundles and lit. The smudge, as the smoking bundle is known, is passed around the people taking part in the ceremony and around the room or the space outside, in order to cleanse and purify the area.

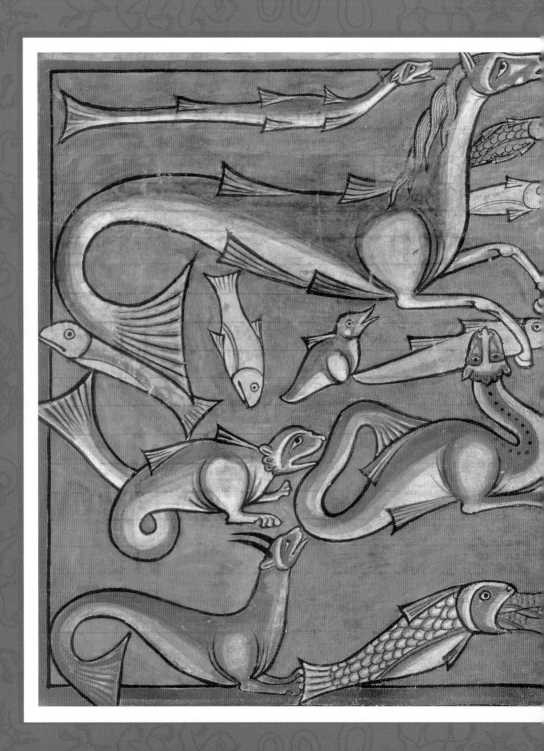

Animal Symbols

Animals hold a central place in the lives of human beings, both practically and symbolically. The close relationships between humans and animals is vividly illustrated in the cave paintings and carvings in France and Spain from 30,000 years ago. These were not aesthetic impressions to be looked at as artistic objects, but were powerful tools. They symbolized a mystical connection to the animal, so that in making an image of their prey, the real animals would succumb to the artist-hunter's power.

During the medieval period in the Christian West, the natural world was seen as a template and source of instruction to humanity. As the Bible said, 'But ask the animals and they will teach you, or the birds of the air, and they will tell you' (Job 12:7–10). They carried the message of God and provided lessons for mankind. This view was developed into a complex mythology about animals and mythical beasts and was incorporated into heraldic coats of arms.

In the 12th century in western Europe there evolved a type of book known as a bestiary in which there were elaborate illustrations of animals and imaginary beasts. In the *Aberdeen Bestiary*, Ms 24, f25v, it explains the purpose of the bestiary as being 'to improve the minds of ordinary people, in such a way that the soul will at least perceive things which it has difficulty grasping mentally; that what they have difficulty comprehending with their ears, they will perceive with their eyes.' The bestiary manuscripts served as a visual language for the largely illiterate public, who knew biblical stories from sermons and could immediately recognize the moral represented by the image of the animal. Later the beasts were formalized on heraldic coats of arms as heraldic animals.

Heraldic Beasts

Heraldry began in order to make it easier to identify participants in jousts, who wore helmets for protection, thereby concealing their faces. Combatants displayed symbols on shields, coats of arms and banners. Many of these symbols are simple colours or shapes, or are marks of cadency, indicating the status of the individual concerned (see pages 224–225) but a third of all arms depict an animal, whether real or mythical, as their charge or as a prominent supporter, each of which has its own significance.

POPULAR CHARGES

The bear, symbolic of strength and a passion for battle, was very popular in Germanic, Celtic and Scandinavian Europe but was surpassed in its popularity during the 12th century CE by the lion, king of beasts, which symbolized valour, strength and royalty. After the lion, the most popular charge was the eagle, king of the skies, which represented immortality, courage, far-sightedness and strength. In modern times, continental European empires have more commonly chosen the eagle as their heraldic emblem: this can be seen on the Polish coat of arms and in the crests of Albania, Romania, the German state of Brandenburg and the arms of the Italian province of South Tyrol. Many heraldic animals bore little resemblance to their real counterparts. The martlet, a common heraldic bird, has not been identified as belonging to one particular species and often appeared stylized, without feet or even a beak. The pike or luce is also depicted as a more generic fish, looking very little like a real pike.

CHARGES AND SOCIAL STANDING

The choice of animal on a coat of ams often corresponded to the social standing of the bearer. Members of the aristocracy commonly included animals they hunted, such as the stag or boar. Domestic animals appear less frequently among the crests of the nobility; dogs and cows are found more commonly on peasants' arms, sheep on the arms of town and religious communities.

MYTHICAL BEASTS

Mythical beasts in heraldry are much more rare than is generally believed. Legendary beasts such as dragons and unicorns, and hybrid creatures, such as sirens or chimeras, entered the bestiary and mythology of heraldry at a relatively late date.

The lion, at one time the most popular heraldic charge, stands for valour and strength.

Heraldic Stances

In heraldry, animals are depicted in stereotypical positions. Four-legged animals are frequently *rampant* – standing on the left hind foot or both hind feet; or *passant* – walking, as in the three-lions coat of arms of the kings of England. The positions below are exemplified by lions.

RAMPANT

The erect lion stands on his hind legs with its front paws raised to strike and with its head in profile, looking forwards. This is the most usual position of a carnivorous quadruped.

PASSANT

This depicts an animal with three legs on the ground, walking. One paw, dexter or right front paw, is raised. The head is in profile and it represents someone who is resolute and determined.

STATANT GUARDANT

This stance depicts an animal standing with all paws on the ground and tail erect. It symbolizes someone able and ready for battle. An animal facing the viewer is *guardant*; looking over its shoulder is *regardant*.

SALIENT

This stance depicts an animal leaping up or springing forward on its prey. It represents someone who will fearlessly push himself into the position of the enemy. It is the emblem of valour.

Heraldic Hunters

In heraldry the bravest, most fearless fighters were symbolized by animals that had the same qualities of courage, strength and determination.

LEOPARD

The leopard is the symbol of a brave warrior who faces dangers with steady courage and does not back away from threat. A *jessant-de-lis*, in which a fleur-de-lis is shooting out of the mouth of a leopard (or lion), symbolizes the dominance of England as the leopard, over France, symbolized by the fleur-de-lis.

WOLF

The crest of the wolf was given as a reward to those who had served in long sieges and had completed difficult enterprises. It represents valour and guardianship. Anyone who bore this symbol would be regarded as one who was dangerous to thwart and would be a deadly enemy.

BEAR

The heraldic bear represents strength, cunning and ferocity in protection of the family. The Viking group called 'Berserkers' wore bear skins in battle and became legendary for their ferocious fighting powers. The bear also symbolizes healing and personal health.

LION

The lion is one of the key animals in heraldry. It is associated with unflinching courage, majesty, prowess in all matters and intelligence. It symbolizes the brave soldier who is sure of his cause and who fights with diligence and fortitude.

Heraldic birds

All heraldic birds carry symbolic meaning and also represent the link between heaven and earth, the spiritual and material worlds.

EAGLE

The eagle is the pre-eminent bird in heraldry, particularly in continental European heraldry. It is a prestigious symbol and represents a brave person of noble birth, and someone who has clear vision in matters of politics and warfare. To pagans it was the emblem of Jupiter, the god of moral law and order. In Rome in 102 BCE the Roman consul Marius decreed that a single-headed eagle should be displayed as the symbol of Imperial Rome.

In modern and medieval heraldry, eagles indicate that the bearer was a wise, courageous man of action. Where the eagle's wings were spread or 'displayed', it indicated the bearer's role as protector. An eagle on a coat of arms indicated a prince of the Holy Roman Empire. The first mention of a double-headed eagle in the West dates from 1250 when it was used by Emperor Frederick II.

The double-headed Seljuk eagle became the symbol of Emperor Michael VIII Palaiologos, who recaptured Constantinople from the Crusaders in 1261. The double head symbolized his interest in both Asia and Europe. An eagle with two heads marks the joining of two forces. Since 1782 the United States of America has used the American bald eagle with wings displayed on its Great Seal.

DOVE

The dove is a symbol of peace and of the Holy Spirit. It represents purity and constancy and, when holding an olive branch, it is the bearer of good news. In heraldry it is always depicted with a small tuft to distinguish it from the wood pigeon. The dove is often found on arms granted to bishops.

DUCK (TEAL)

Ducks evade their enemies by flying, running, swimming or diving and symbolize a person who is resourceful and skilful in battle. As with all birds they symbolize mediation between Heaven and Earth, between the spiritual and material worlds.

FALCON (HAWK)

The falcon represents someone who does not rest until his mission is completed. It is often found on the arms of noble families that date from the time when falcons were used in hunting. It is a symbol of majesty and power. When at rest on its perch, the falcon symbolizes that the bearer of the coat of arms is ready and capable of carrying out service in matters of high state.

GOOSE

To the Celts the goose symbolized prophetic knowledge, bloodshed and skill and was seen as the messenger of the gods. The wild goose was the symbol of the God Spirit, and bones of geese have been unearthed in the graves of Iron Age Celtic warriors.

MARTLET

The footless bird represents ceaseless flight and swiftness, and the qualities of the sure soldier who will not rest until victory is achieved. Following his wars on France, this symbol was bestowed by Edward III on those knights whose valour secured victory.

OSTRICH

The ostrich symbolizes faith and contemplation, truth and justice. It was domesticated by the early Romans who used ostriches to pull their triumphal chariots, and since that time the ostrich has been associated with willing obedience and serenity.

PARROT

The parrot, sometimes called a 'popinjay' in heraldry, may represent someone who has given distinguished service in a tropical country. It is found in early English and French heraldry.

PEACOCK

The peacock is associated with beauty, power and knowledge. In Christian symbolism it represents the soul and resurrection, since in ancient times it was believed that the flesh of the peacock could not decay and was everlasting. Also, the 'hundred eyes' in the peacock's tail signified the all-seeing Church.

RAVEN

Attracted to shiny objects, the raven represents the desire for knowledge and independent pursuit of personal desires. It also symbolizes a strategist in battle and divine providence. The raven on a coat of arms indicates that the bearer has achieved fortune by his own efforts.

PELICAN

The pelican is the Christian symbol of self-sacrifice and charity. It signifies parental love and devotion to offspring. It is said to feed its young with its own blood, though in reality it retrieves previously caught small fish from a sack in its skin. This seemingly selfless act and the reddish colour of some plumage symbolizes Christ's sacrifice. In heraldic terms the pelican represents one who will sacrifice himself for the greater good.

CRANE (STORK)

The crane is a sacred bird. According to myth, cranes lived in social groups and took turns in standing watch. The sentry crane held a stone, known as the vigilance, in one claw so that if it fell asleep the stone would drop and wake him. It symbolizes vigilance, protection and close familial bonds, especially between parent and child.

SWAN

The swan represents harmony, grace, sincerity and devotion. It is the sign of poets and musicians and those who love learning. In Ireland, the swan was said to carry the soul of the dead Celtic chieftain to the next life. A cygnet, a young swan, with a crown around its neck, symbolizes dignity.

COCK

The cock tells time, heralds the dawn and symbolizes watchfulness. It represents courage, perseverance and a man in politics. Cocks fight with each other for supremacy and the defeated cock no longer crows, so the triumphant cock signals a hero in the field of battle.

Heraldic Fish and Aquatic Creatures

Symbolic of the forces of industry and science and used by military families to indicate prowess and fortitude, heraldic dolphins and sea monsters were also frequently used to decorate and illustrate maps.

DOLPHIN

The dolphin is the symbol of safe travel as well as swiftness, salvation, charity and love. Older heralds regarded it as the king of fish, just as the lion is known as the king of beasts and the eagle as the king of birds. It was known as the sailor's friend and said to be devoted to saving lives. In Christian symbolism it represents Christ who guides lost souls across the water of death.

WHALE

The size of the whale, like a mountain in the sea, led some sailors into mistaking it for land. According to legend they would anchor, climb on to the back of the whale and even build fires to cook on; however, when the whale plunged below, they were thrown to their deaths. Thus the whale came to signify evil and was used as a symbol of the devil.

PIKE (LUCE)

'Luce' comes from the Latin *lucius*, which derives from the Greek word for wolf. The pike is viewed as the wolf of the sea. It is the symbol of prowess and fortitude in battle and is associated with military families. It also symbolizes a true, generous mind and, as a fish was the emblem used by early Christians, it is a sign of unity and spiritual nourishment.

BEAVER

The beaver, known for its building ability, represents industry and perseverance. It is an emblem of cooperation and community. In Christian symbolism the beaver represents chastity. It is also the sign of vigilance and self-sacrifice and is used in heraldry to represent protection and dedication.

OTTER

The otter is a symbol of grace and empathy. The bearer of this symbol is industrious, persevering and has the ability to play, someone who lives his life to the full. It is found widely on Scottish and Irish coats of arms.

LOBSTER AND CRAYFISH

Lobsters are rare in heraldry, with crayfish and crabs appearing more frequently. It is often unclear, however, which animal is being depicted, so that blazons sometimes name the charge crab, crayfish, lobster or even scorpion. Lobsters were thought to be the enemy of serpents and, as serpents are associated with sin, were subsequently seen as a symbol of temperance.

HERRING

This fish was used mainly as a pun, as it appears on the shields of families with similar-sounding names. It represents good health, hospitality and financial security, particularly for families of fishermen.

Heraldic Domestic Animals

Heraldic domestic animals represent the taming of wild creatures so that their abilities can be harnessed for human benefit.

DOG

The dog is an emblem of fidelity, courage and vigilance. The Talbot symbolizes an English hunting dog and represents a skilled hunter, and is found on the coats of arms of great hunting families.

CAT

A symbol of a great cat, such as a puma, wildcat or mountain cat or mountain lion, represents liberty, vigilance and courage. Cats are mainly found on Scottish and Irish coats of arms.

HORSE

A medieval knight needed at least four different types of horse: a charger, a palfrey, a courser and a battle horse. The horse symbolized readiness of service for king and country and represented strength, devotion and steadfastness.

BULL

A bull or ox represents valour, bravery and generosity. The horns symbolize strength and fortitude. It is a symbol of the Sun and masculine energy.

Heraldic Animals of the Fields and Forest

Animals of field and forest symbolize the importance of the natural world in the lives of human beings.

FOX

In the Middle Ages the fox was commonly regarded as a symbol of the devil and in a coat of arms it signified that the bearer was ever-vigilant against evil. The fox is one of the most famous tricksters and represents someone who will use wit and quick thinking to achieve his objective or to defend himself.

HARE

This heraldic symbol signifies someone who enjoys a peaceful, retired life. However, as hares, like rabbits, are noted for their reproductive abundance, they have become symbols of lusty fertility.

BADGER

The badger is noted for its fierceness and courage in defending its home. It represents bravery, perseverance and protection and is found widely on coats of arms.

BEE

The bee is a symbol of industry, hard work, creativity and diligence. In heraldry it is used to represent well-regulated industry. The bee is the most popular insect in heraldry and is usually shown with a beehive.

STAG (HART)

The stag is a symbol of strength and virility, purity and fleetness. Throughout the world the hart or deer represents transformation, regeneration and spirituality. It is a Moon symbol and relates to fertility. The antlers are shed annually and regrow, making it a token of rebirth and life after death.

In Christianity, the stag is the symbol for Christ, who tramples on the devil and brings redemption through death and resurrection. The person bearing this symbol was considered to be impervious to the weapons of others. The stag's antlers link it to the Tree of Life, which features in so many religious traditions. The Celts believed that deer were tribes of fairies or divinities, and the antlered 'Horned God' was the supreme power over all the animals.

BUCK

The buck represents the male deer and symbolizes someone who will not initiate a fight, but will respond if provoked. It signifies someone who desires peace and harmony. In Ireland the buck was one of the most ancient charges and represented the ancestors of the Celtic race.

BOAR

The boar is known for its bravery and capacity to fight to the death. It is a fierce combatant and is used in coats of arms to symbolize valiant warriors. In Ireland, the boar is a popular charge, probably because the meat was considered to be the food of the Celtic gods; a symbol of the boar was worn as a charm against injury during battle. The boar's head represents hospitality or one who is hospitable.

ELEPHANT

In heraldic symbolism the elephant represents great strength, loyalty, longevity, happiness and ambition. Elephants in the East carry kings and queens and so are associated with royalty and nobility. On coats of arms the elephant signifies a person of dignity, wisdom and reliability. It is a very auspicious symbol. The elephant symbolizes power and determination to succeed.

SNAKE

The snake or serpent is a common symbol in heraldry, where it may be called a serpent, cobra, adder or bis. It is associated with the caduceus and healing as it was sacred to Asklepios, the god of healing. The snake symbolizes death and rebirth as it sheds its skin and continues life. Because of its forked tongue the snake is linked to lightning and the Sun and it represents the bearer's ability to make lightning strikes when provoked. It symbolizes wisdom, cunning and mystical insight.

TORTOISE

The tortoise or turtle represents longevity, patience and sagacity. In the 17th and 18th centuries it was a source of meat for sailors, who valued its strength and its independence since it carried its home on its back. It is a symbol of protection because of its hard shell and indicates invulnerability under attack. The name 'tortoise', Latin *testuoo*, was given to an ancient Roman manoeuvre which provided soldiers with protection when they overlapped their shields above their heads when engaged in warfare. The Chinese Imperial army carried a dragon and tortoise banner to signify indestructibility. The tortoise was the symbol of Aphrodite/Venus, and also often accompanied Mercury, the messenger god, who was said to have invented the lyre from a tortoise shell.

Mythical Beasts

There is a whole array of mythical beasts, made up of an amalgamation of real animals and fantastical creatures with symbolic powers. Chimerical monsters are composites of different parts of different beasts and mythical creatures. In heraldry the term 'heraldic monster' describes any creature not found in nature, in other words, a fabulous beast.

The combination of different animals, natural and mythical, gave great creative freedom to their inventors. Unleashed from convention, they could create fabulous beasts and include whatever characteristics they wanted. These amalgams symbolized the chaos of the world and the vagaries of the natural world, which could alter man's life in the blink of an eyelid. In heraldry, these winged monsters sometimes sit on either side of the charge to indicate protection from such threats.

In a Chinese myth which describes the creation of the universe, P'an Ku, the first god/human, took 18,000 years to complete the task and was aided by the four most fortunate animals, the dragon, the phoenix, the tortoise and the unicorn. These sacred animals became the guardians of the hidden realms of the Earth and beyond, and they feature in heraldic coats of arms.

Unicorns are widely found on coats of arms and are symbolic of purity and innocence.

GRIFFIN

The mythical griffin has four feet, the hind legs of a lion, with the wings, talons and head of an eagle. It is composed of the most noble bird and king of the beasts. It combines the strength and power of the lion's terrestrial powers and the celestial powers of flight and keen vision of the eagle. This combination makes it a significant symbol of the power of salvation. It represents their qualities of death-defying bravery, excellent vision and tenacity as well as valour.

The griffin was believed to guard goldmines and hidden treasure and thus symbolized the vigilance of the arms bearer. It is the enemy of the horse and is often depicted grasping an ox or other animal and striking an heraldic pose with one foot raised. A *rampant* griffin is termed *sergeant*, and the heraldic keythong is a male griffin, represented as wingless, but with either spikes of fur or jets of flame or light coming from the main body area.

The gryphon was a symbol of Persia and its main religion Zoroastrianism. It represents the valiant soldier who will do anything to avoid capture. In the East, the gryphon, like the dragon, symbolizes wisdom. In ancient Greece it was identified with monsters that guarded the treasure of the Hyperboreans and is often depicted in this way.

DRAGON

In heraldry, the dragon has the head of a serpent with forked ears and tongue, the body of a lion with scales, large wings and webbed talons for feet. The word is derived from the Greek and means 'to see clearly', which is sometimes interpreted as the gift of prophecy. The dragon symbolizes the absolute defender of anything that is treasured. It is a symbol of a valiant defender who is brave and protective. The dragon's strength is in its tail, which it lashes about and is linked to volatility and a fiery nature.

The devil is compared to the dragon because he is the worst of all the serpents. The dragon also stands for the universe itself which no one can ever fully master.

CHIMERA

The chimera, whose name means 'she-goat', has the head, mane and legs of a lion, the body of a goat and the pointed tail of a dragon. It breathed hot fire and in medieval times represented all the forces of Satan. It is the symbol of evil and danger on land and at sea. In medieval times it represented lust and sexual desire.

CENTAUR

Centaurs are seen in classical Greek mythology as a half man, half horse and are used as heraldic beasts. Some people believe the idea came from the horsemen of the Thessalians, because in battle, on horseback, they were so perfectly attuned that horse and man seemed as one. It symbolizes strength and speed.

ENFIELD

A mythical beast with the head and ears of a fox, chest of a greyhound, forelegs of an eagle, body of a lion and hind legs and tail of a wolf. In myth it is supposed to have protected a fallen chieftain's body until a proper burial could take place.

ALERION

A mythical creature similar to an eagle, but without talons or beak, the alerion is commonly depicted with its wings outstretched, or 'displayed'. It symbolizes a bearer who was injured in battle and who was unable to assert his full skills as a warrior. It also represents strength of will and intellectual ability.

PHOENIX

The phoenix is a bird from Greek mythology that was consumed in flames, but rose from its own ashes. In myth the phoenix lived for a hundred years, then laid an egg, which it hatched by setting fire to itself. It symbolizes immortality, resurrection and renewal. The phoenix is also a symbol of love. Modern heralds emblazon the phoenix as a demi-eagle.

UNICORN

Predominantly depicted as white with a single horn, the unicorn has the body of a horse, the tale of a lion and the legs of an antelope. It is associated with purity and innocence; unicorns are linked with virgins as it was believed only a virgin could catch or tame this elusive creature. In Christian iconography it is a sign of the incarnation of Christ, the one horn symbolizing the doctrine that Christ is one with God.

CHINESE UNICORN

In Chinese illustrations, the great unicorn or *qi'lin* is shown with the body of a deer with white or yellow fur and symbolizes times of peace and prosperity. It was said to avoid fighting at all costs and walked so softly its hooves made no sound. People believed that this was because it was so gentle-hearted it did not want to hurt a blade of grass beneath its feet. It also represents the reign of a wise emperor. In Chinese mythology it is said that the sovereign Fu Hsi (*c.*2900 BCE) was wondering how to record his history, since writing had not yet been invented, when the *qi'lin* rose out of the river and came towards him with certain magical signs on his back. From these Fu Hsi was then able to devise the Chinese system of writing based on the Pa Kua or eight trigrams, which later became the *I Ching* or *Book of Changes*.

COCKATRICE

Half fowl and half reptile, a cockatrice is similar to a wyvern (see page 205) but has a cockscomb, wattles and a barbed tongue.

The cockatrice was believed to come from a hen's egg hatched by a serpent and was a terror to all who beheld it. This creature would also be referred to heraldically as a basilisk, wyvern or dragon. The Greek name *basiliscus* means 'little king' and its odour is said to kill snakes. It can also kill by hissing, which is why it is called the *sibilus*. A person who bore this symbol aimed to instil terror in his enemies, though it was also a sign of protection to his followers. Like Medusa in Greek mythology, the cockatrice could turn to stone anyone who looked at it.

MERMAID (SIREN)

The mermaid or merman symbolizes anything related to seafaring or the sea. The siren was an alternative name for a mermaid and a triton was a merman. The mermaid is usually shown with a mirror, symbol of imagination and truth, and a hairbrush in her hands. Sirens are symbols of eloquence since the song of siren was so beautiful it lured sailors to their deaths. The *museline* is a mermaid with two tails, one on each side, and is favoured in German heraldry.

SALAMANDER

The salamander symbolizes someone of good faith. It appears as a lizard and is usually shown surrounded by flames since it was believed that it walked through fire, protecting itself by oozing a milky substance that insulated its skin. It is a sign of courage. It appeared on the coat of arms of Francis I of France as a symbol of the patron of good things and the destroyer of bad. In the Christian religion it is a symbol of a true believer who resists the fire of temptation.

MANTICORE (MAN-TIGER)

This mythical beast has the body of an heraldic tiger and the head of an old man, sometimes depicted with long spiral horns coming from the forehead. It symbolizes someone who is wise and knowledgeable, but who will fight with unremitting fierceness.

HIPPOGRIFF

This mythical beast has the head, wings and fore claws of a female griffin and the hind parts of a horse. It represents someone who has shown great courage in the protection of home and family.

WYVERN

The mythical two-legged winged dragon with a serpent's tail symbolizes valour and protection. Gifted with excellent vision, it is charged with guarding treasure. The bearer of this symbol would be regarded as a strong defender of people and property. It also signifies vigilance and perseverance.

SEA DOG

The sea dog represented sea ports and sailors who spend their life at sea. It is part of the family of sea chimeras, such as the mermaid, sea lion and the heraldic sea horse.

$\mathscr{S}$YMBOLS OF POWER

Symbols of power – religious, political and military – have been used in all societies since people began to believe in gods and to follow rulers. Sovereigns, whether benign or dictatorial, used symbols to emphasize their authority, as did officers of the Church and the military. Power had to be seen and felt in all places so that the populace knew who was in charge and what was expected of them; thus easily understood symbols of power, such as the mace, were placed in sacred and important buildings. Some symbols of power are attached to ritual and ceremony, while others are significant militarily or politically.

Many symbols of power have evolved out of warfare and combat. Heads of state and sovereigns have adopted ancient symbols to create a mystique of authority and power. The mace, the sword and the baton all have a place in military history as real weapons, although these days when worn or carried in ceremonies, they may represent past and present military and political prowess. Religious symbols, too, hark back to ancient times: the bishop's mitre and crosier, the papal keys and cross have an ancient significance that still speaks volumes to those who use them and those who observe and witness their use.

Royalty and the Church

The coronation of the sovereign in many cultures and countries takes the form of an initiation ceremony, in which the new monarch is crowned and invested with the regalia, the privileges and insignia of office. It includes all the major symbols that denote the power of the monarchy.

In many instances, the highest-ranking officer of the Church performs this ceremony, at which specific robes with historical and symbolic meaning are worn. Cloaks, capes and gowns are sometimes embellished with powerful symbols or trimmed with fur, or coloured in such a way as to represent power – ermine and the colour purple being two examples of regal symbols.

SYMBOLS IN THE CHURCH

The Christian Church is also rich in powerful symbols tied to its rituals; from the ordination of priests to the anointing of bishops and popes, each ceremony and each position has its own collection of ancient and meaningful symbols.

Christianity is found all over the world and most of its followers choose Protestantism or Roman Catholicism, the denominations most associated with ceremony and symbolism. The chief Christian symbol is the cross, which signifies the crucifixion of Christ. Over 2,000 years, leaders of Christianity have developed a hierarchy that is revealed in the form of majestic cathedrals, elaborate rituals and symbolic objects such as the crosier and orb. The symbols of power can be seen as a form of demarcation, those who are initiated into the inner mysteries of faith – priests – carrying symbols of power while others look on in wonder. Those who seek spiritual guidance from the church look to those symbols and find comfort and protection.

This portrait depicts Charlemagne with numerous symbols of power: an orb, sceptre and crown. The bejewelled robe also indicates his high status.

CROWN

This is an emblem of sovereignty and victory and evolved from the double diadem of the Egyptian pharaohs. The circle of the crown signifies perfection and continuity. Crowns were made of laurel leaves and given to victors in the ancient Olympic games. The 'crowning achievement' represents success and supremacy.

DIADEM

Originally from the Greek *diadein* meaning 'to bind or fasten', the diadem in its first form was a white ribbon tied with a knot around the head of the king, with two strips resting on the shoulders. It was a symbol of authority and the mark of the leader.

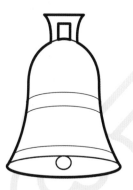

BELL

The bell signifies the power of the Church to disperse evil spirits and call the faithful to prayer. A Canterbury bell was a symbol of pilgrimage. The Celtic bell, Bellenos, known also as the Brilliant One, was a solar deity linked to Apollo.

KEYS

Keys are the symbol of the authority of the papacy and the Church's power to lock people into its teachings. In the Bible, St Peter is given the keys to Heaven by Christ, which symbolizes the connection between Heaven and Earth.

CROSIER

The crosier represents those in high office in the Church. The shepherd's crosier signifies the shepherd's watchfulness as he cares for his flock. The crosier is the symbol of the office of a bishop and he carries it whenever he is giving sacraments or leading worship.

The pointed ferule at the base symbolizes the right of the prelate to prod those who are not as spiritually active as they should be. The crook signifies his responsibility to gather in those who have strayed off the religious path and the staff represents his duty to stand firm and support the members of his flock.

The crosier symbol appeared in the early Neolithic period carved on menhirs and was used in ancient Egypt and Rome. It was adopted by the Christian Church and is represented in the stylized staff carried by Roman Catholic, Eastern Orthodox, Anglican and Lutheran prelates. The crosier is presented to an abbot at his dedication as a symbol that he is the shepherd whose duty it is to tend his community of monks in the monastery.

A crosier appears on ecclesiastic coats of arms of cardinals, nuns, bishops and others holding positions of power within the Church, to signify their authority. In Eastern Christianity when a new bishop is consecrated he is presented with a crosier.

RING

Rings are worn by those in religious office. The ring a bishop wears symbolizes his union with the Church, while the ring that a nun wears represents her marriage to God.

The papal ring or 'Fisherman's Ring' is bestowed when a pope is anointed and is broken on his death.

PAPAL CROSS

The official symbol of the papacy, this three-barred cross represents the Trinity of the Father, Son and Holy Spirit. It originated in the Cross of Lorraine, which has two horizontals and was used by bishops in medieval Christianity.

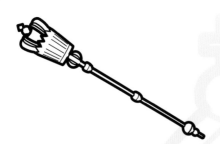

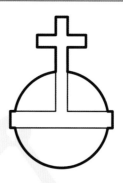

MACE

The mace is a significant symbol of absolute authority in judicial, political and religious settings. It is often a short, highly decorated staff with a knob at the top and decorated with a coat of arms. A ceremonial mace was carried in front of a sovereign or a high official. In papal chapels the club-shaped mace or *mazza* is carried by papal mace-bearers. In times past the mace-bearers were the pope's bodyguards, a custom that dates back to the 12th century.

ORB

The orb is a religious and royal symbol consisting of a ball surmounted by a cross. The round orb represents the Earth and, surmounted by a cross, it signifies the Church's Christian power over the material world. It is held in the monarch's left hand, making it a feminine symbol, unlike the sceptre, a masculine symbol, which is always held in the right.

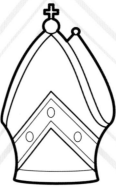

MITRE

A bishop's mitre symbolizes religious authority. It derives from the headgear of high priests of pre-Christian Rome, which was in the shape of a fish head. The high priest Pontifex Maximus wore a conical mitre called an apex whenever he was outdoors, which symbolized spiritual power descending from Heaven into his head.

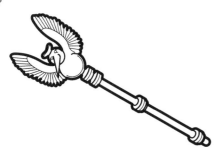

SCEPTRE

The sceptre comes from a Greek work signifying a rod or staff. Originally it symbolized that the chief or king was like a shepherd to his people. To ancient Egyptians it was a symbol of domination and power. It is often shown being carried by gods to signify their supreme authority. The sceptre represents royal power, justice, sovereignty and is the emblem of the Archangel Gabriel.

In Japan the *nyoi* depicts authority and is carried by abbots. In Buddhism the *dorje*, the 'noble stone', is a sceptre or rod that represents the highest authority. The diamond sceptre, the adamantine or 'thunderbolt' symbolizes the divine force of the Buddhist teaching.

SWORD

The sword is a symbol of the Passion of Christ and the emblem of Archangel Michael. A flaming sword at each corner separates man from Paradise. At the coronation of a British sovereign the Sword of State is presented. Later the king or queen is given the Sword of Spiritual Justice, the Sword of Temporal Justice and the Sword of Mercy.

SCALLOP SHELL

The scallop shell is the symbol of pilgrimage. It was the symbol of St James, the patron saint of pilgrims. Pilgrims often wore scallop shell shaped brooches or pendants. It was worn by Christians to indicate completion of the pilgrimage to the shrine of St James of Compostela in Spain. The scallop is also the symbol of baptism and is frequently carved or painted on baptismal fonts. The dish used by priests to pour water over the baby's head is usually in the shape of a scallop.

Military Symbols

Military symbols reflect the authority and power of the forces that strive to maintain peace and protect the inhabitants of the country they serve. Discipline within the ranks, a strict code of conduct and ceremonial parades all have military symbols that represent duties and allegiances.

RANK

Symbols of military rank and power can be seen on military uniforms. For instance, by 1800 a crossed sword and baton device was used to denote the rank of general in the British Army, and the different grades of generals were further indicated by the number and groupings of buttons on their coats. Badges for field officers consist of crowns and stars and were first introduced in 1810. Originally insignia indicating rank was worn on the collar, but was moved to the shoulders in 1880 for all officers. Today there is a complex system of markings, which are on braids around the cuffs as well as on epaulettes.

REWARD

The 'fesse' (a broad horizontal band across a shield) is used in heraldry and represents a military belt or girdle of honour. It was given by kings and emperors to reward special services performed by soldiers.

Chevrons are worn on uniforms as a symbol of protection and are granted to those military personnel who have carried out notable actions. Ribbons, like chevrons, are bestowed as a reward for outstanding military activity and are attached to medals. The colour and design have special significance: the purple ribbon for the Purple Heart and red, white and blue ribbon for the Distinguished Service Medal, both awarded in the US.

As with medals throughout the world, these Russian ones symbolize military prowess.

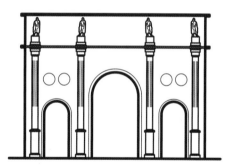

ACORN

The oak tree, a symbol of strength, honour, endurance and stability, plays a part in military symbolism. The tree, the oak leaves and acorn signify power, authority and victory and are often displayed on military tombs.

ARCHES

The arched ceremonial gateway signifies transformation, being born again. The Roman triumphal arch symbolizes military victory. Arches may be double or single and signify a governor or magistrate.

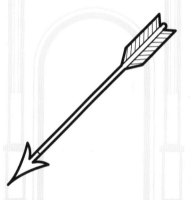

ARROWS AND ARROWHEADS

Throughout history the arrow has been a symbol of speed, power and swift response to attack. It is the emblem of the Greek god Apollo and the goddess Artemis, both associated with hunting. Cheyenne warriors, known for their fearless battle prowess, regarded their medicine arrows as symbols of male power. Used in military iconography, arrows represent readiness for martial combat and military defence.

BATTLEAXE

Axes have had military and religious significance since the Neolithic period. Changes were made to simple axes to enhance their mystical power and raise the status of the owner. Some of these early unshafted axes that have been found in archaeological digs show no sign of wear and may have been thought of a gifts from the gods. For the Celts, the axe symbolized a divine being, a chief or a warrior. The battle-axe represents authority and the execution of military duty. First used as a military symbol in the Crusades, it continues to represent power in conflict.

BANNER

The banner is a flag painted, dyed or embroidered with the arms of the owner. The larger the banner, the more important the rank of the bearer. It is a symbol of victory and in some heraldic coats of arms a banner will be depicted in the design. Banners were presented after a particularly significant military action had taken place. Sometimes they are shown because an ancestor was a standard-bearer and carried the banner into battle. On the battleground, the banner symbolized a rallying point, physically and psychologically.

SCALES

Scales or balances are traditionally associated with justice. The Scales of Justice are used today to signify an unbiased judicial system.

CALTRAP

The caltrap, galtrap or the cheval trap was an ancient instrument of war. It had four points and, when thrown to the earth, three points pointed upwards, making it a deadly weapon for enemies on foot or on horseback. It symbolizes an awesome warrior.

CEREMONIAL MACE

The ceremonial mace was an early symbol of the authority of military commanders. As the earliest maces were weapons to protect the sovereign, they were carried by the sergeants-at-arms, the king's bodyguards. By the 14th century they had become elaborately decorated objects and were a symbol of power rather than a weapon.

SWORD

The dual symbolism of the sword is apparent in its use as a military weapon and in its defence of land, family or fortune. Swords were so finely crafted and balanced that

some were said to have magical powers, such as Excalibur, the sword of King Arthur. The sword is the symbol of military honour and is associated with justice, liberty and strength. In England, it is used in the ceremonial knighting of those who have given outstanding service to queen and country. The sword represents the higher order of knights, while the lance represents the lower ranks.

In the Crusades the sword had ceremonial importance as well as military significance. In Japan, a sword is one of the Three Treasures of the Japanese emperor, while in Buddhism the sword is attributed with the ability to cut through ignorance.

FASCES

A bundle of rods tied together around an axe, with the blade projecting out, is symbolic of a magistrate's authority and the judiciary. The rods symbolize the power of the state to punish wrongdoers and the axe represents the ultimate power – that is, the ability to execute those who transgress. Many governments and military institutions, dating back to the Roman Empire, have used the image of the fasces as a symbol of power. Roman soldiers would carry them in public ceremonies and inspections. Italian fascism took its name from the fasces. The symbol represents strength though unity, since the bundle has more power than one rod on its own.

The coat of arms of the Swiss canton of St Gallen has displayed fasces since 1803. It is also on the front cover of French passports and has been incorporated into many insignia. It appears on the state seal of Colorado, USA, below the all-seeing eye, and is on the seal of the New York borough of Brooklyn.

SHIELD

Shields are used as protection against missiles and hand blows and have been made of wood, animal skins, metal and even turtle shells. They vary according to the role of the soldier: small round *aspis* were used by the ancient Greeks when speed was essential, while Roman legionaries carried *scuta*, large rectangular shields, vital in heavy bombardment, but not built for speed. Some were designed with a recess to carry the spear so that soldiers could create a wall of shields. Free-standing shields known as *pavises* were used by medieval crossbow warriors to protect them when they were reloading.

The shield is used in coats of arms and military units have their own symbols to represent their particular skills. The crest of the Pershing Rifles has a blue shield on which are crossed rifles and a torch. The torch is the symbol of readiness to meet any situation, in any place, and it denotes high achievement in scholarship. The crossed rifles are a symbol of power and military strength in upholding peace.

Shields are still used today by police and military personnel in riot control, mainly transparent ones so that they can see the rioters, or in the form of body armour made of Lexan or Mylar.

HAMMER AND SICKLE

The hammer symbolizes the duality of male energy – that it can be used to create and build or destroy. It is the emblem of the Norse god Thor, who used it to kill and to create valleys from solid mountains. The hammer also represents industriousness, while the sickle is an emblem of agriculture. The hammer and sickle were the emblem of Soviet Russia and symbolized fruitful industry.

LANCE

This masculine symbol represents solar rays, as do arrows and swords. The lance is a phallic symbol sometimes known as a blade and is paired with the cup or chalice, to represent the union of male and female and the Holy Grail. It is associated with chivalry, though knights who hired themselves as warriors, similar to mercenaries today, were called 'freelance'. The lance is a symbol of victory and is the emblem of the Hindu god of war Indra. A broken lance is a symbol of St George, who used a lance to slay the dragon. It is also the symbol of an experienced soldier.

TRIDENT

The trident represents dominion over the seas and sea power. It was the symbol of the Greek god of the sea Poseidon (Neptune in Roman mythology), and the three prongs represented forked lightning.

BATON

The word 'baton' comes from the French for stick and has come to represent authority. In Roman times a military legate was given a short white baton as a symbol of the Imperial power entrusted to him. At the ceremony where he was invested with the baton, the legate held it above his head declaring, 'Above your head and mine', invoking his right to represent the authority of the emperor which no one could challenge.

CREST

Knights wore crests on their helmets to symbolize the object of their quests or to identify where their allegiances lay. Military units each have their own unique crest.

SIGNET RING

The signet ring was a symbol of power and authority. It was used to make an impression, which indicated authenticity, and such rings were first used in ancient Greece. It symbolized designated authority as the ring could be passed from one person to another.

Heraldry

Heraldry is both an art and a science. It originated from the need to recognize participants and opponents in jousts between knights, whose faces would be covered by steel visors. Later knights wore special badges and carried banners to identify themselves and had their own colours and symbols. The designs on the shields were also put on sleeveless coats, surcoats, which were the first coats of arms. Heraldry is the name given to the study of these symbols and patterns and to the rules governing their use.

In early battles, messengers or heralds recorded the designs worn by the combatants, so they could communicate the outcome of the battles. These heraldic records became the authority that stipulated which symbols and colours could be used by which families on their coats of arms and other armorial bearings such as banners and pennants.

The design on the coat of arms is called the 'charge', and the simplest are known as ordinaries (stripes, crosses). Sometimes the charge might be an animal such as a lion, gryphon or dragon (see Heraldic Beasts, pages 186–199).

In the USA the word 'crest' is used instead of coat of arms; however, crest in the UK is just one part of the complete 'achievement of arms' – the crest is placed on top of a helmet. The main part of the arms is the shield or escutcheon, which is often held up by supporters, upon which may be mythical beasts; a family motto may be found beneath the shield.

HEREDITY

The nobility in Britain were the first to use personal badges to signify their name and status. By the time Henry III was on the throne, coats of arms were inherited and it was necessary to ensure their systematization and regulation. The importance of marks of cadency, to indicate the status of the sons in a family and to distinguish one son from another, was standardized by the 15th century. In the late Middle Ages heraldry was a well-established discipline, regulated by professional heralds. Coats of arms would be included on banners, carved in wood, embroidered on garments, in stained-glass windows and wherever the family wanted to display its 'brand'. Coats of arms and their accessories are described as 'blazon'.

These elements used in French heraldry show a variety of simple 'ordinaries' used on coats of arms.

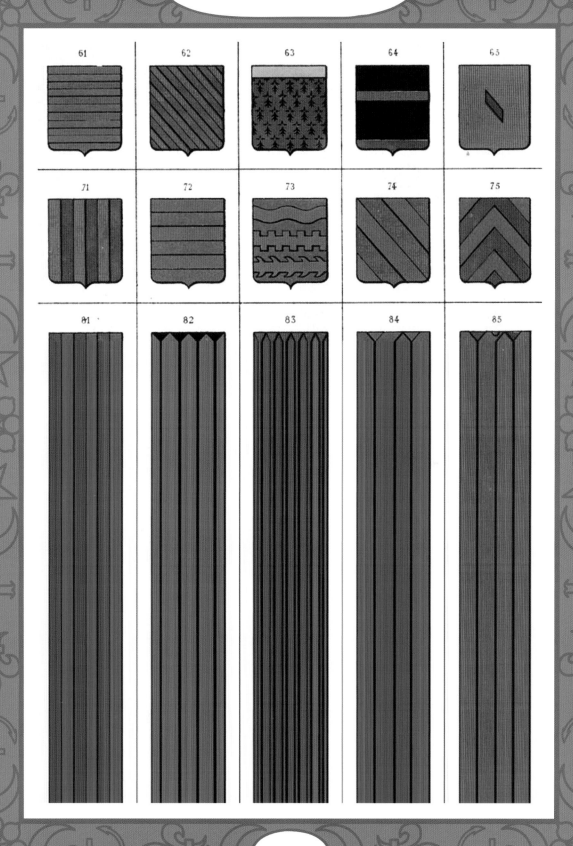

Marks of Cadency

The original idea for coats of arms was to distinguish one knight from another, and later it was important to distinguish different members of the same family who had the right to bear paternal arms. A system known as marks of cadency or differences was devised. These marks were added to the original coat of arms as follows:

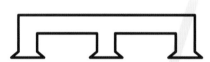

LABEL OF THREE POINTS –
ELDEST SON, THE FIRST-BORN
DURING THE LIFETIME OF
HIS FATHER

CRESCENT – SECOND SON

MULLET – THIRD SON

MARTLET – FOURTH SON

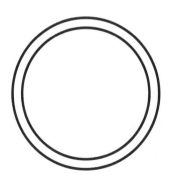

ANNULET – FIFTH SON

FLEUR-DE-LIS – SIXTH SON

ROSE – SEVENTH SON

CROSS MOLINE – EIGHTH SON

ANCHOR – NINTH SON

DOUBLE QUATREFOIL – TENTH SON

Tincture

An important aspect of heraldry is that of colour or, to use the correct heraldic term, 'tincture'. The tinctures had special names and because of the early need for swift recognition of the wearer, six main colours were used: yellow, white, red, blue, black and green. Purple, though it counted in theory, was rarely used in practice. The metals were gold and silver, and each colour and metal carried symbolic meaning.

METALS

GOLD (OR)
Generosity and elevation of the mind

SILVER/WHITE (ARGENT)
Peace, sincerity

COLOURS

RED (GULES)
Sign of a warrior or martyr.
Courage, military strength
and generosity

BLUE (AZURE)
Truth and loyalty

BLACK (SABLE)
Constancy or grief

PURPLE (PURPURE)
Sovereignty, royalty
and justice

WHITE
Honour

GREEN (VERT)
Hope, joy and loyalty

Fur

As well as the solid tinctures, certain patterns called 'furs' were used and function in the same way, being easily recognized as representing a particular family. Two common furs are ermine and vair.

ERMINE

Ermine is the most widely used fur in heraldry and is the winter coat of the stoat, which is white with a black tail. The heraldic fur is a white base with a pattern of black spots. The ermine was believed to be so concerned about its pure-white coat that it would die rather than become soiled – this came to symbolize the Christian's desire to die rather than sin, and is also associated with dignity. Clerics and royalty wore ermine fur as a sign of piety.

VAIR

This represents a type of squirrel with a blue-grey back and a white belly; joined together, they give a pattern of alternating blue and white shapes.

SHIELD AND LOZENGE

The shape of the shield is varied, both in heraldry and in those used in battle. The shield is the shape that carried the design called a 'charge'. Over time, instead of being tall and rectangular, it became shorter. The simplest shield designs are called 'ordinaries'. When heraldry was first established women did not go to war and so technically did not have shields on which to put their coat of arms. Instead their emblems were depicted on a lozenge shape, a rhombus standing on one of its acute corners, except in the case of a queen or empress, who, for legal reasons, was viewed as male.

Only the king could grant permission to carry a coat of arms; though initially granted only to knights and noble families, this was later extended to merchants or craftsmen. Their charge would show their trade – for example, a barrel for a wine merchant.

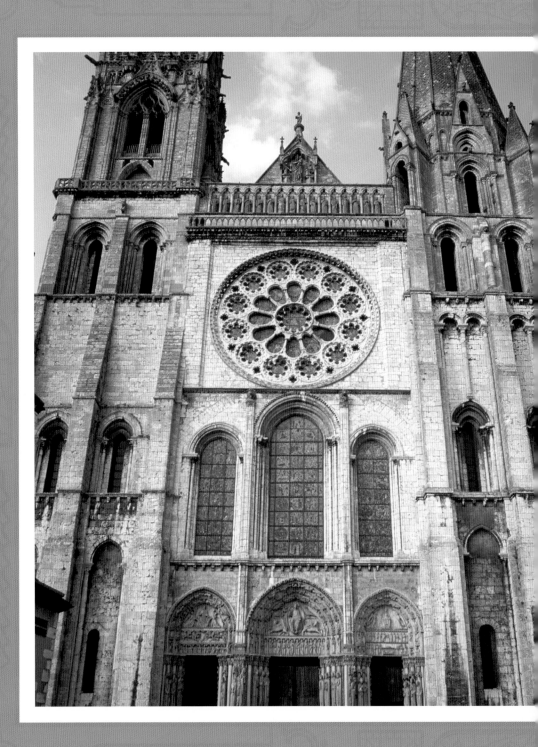

SACRED ARCHITECTURE

Architect and astrologer A T Mann wrote that 'sacred architecture is an integration of space and time, Earth and Heaven and at its most profound, accesses the timeless'. In ancient times, sacred buildings aligned with the stars and the axis oriented towards the rising Sun. Later temples were erected to mark these sacred sites – the word *templum* means a place where stellar observations are made.

The site chosen for a sacred building is often a power spot – *hsueh*, over a leyline, or natural water course. *Hsuehs* or dragons' nests are places where the Earth's natural energy is highly concentrated. The cardinal points or directions are a primary source of spiritual power, which is why the orientation towards the horizon is so important in sacred architecture.

In Asia the whole landscape is considered sacred and architecture is regarded as a divine science.

Buildings are constructed using divine geometric proportions together with geomancy, the art of placing buildings on auspicious sites.

The temple, mosque, church and synagogue are all places of worship, where set rituals and ceremonies are performed. In designing sacred buildings the architect must bear in mind what will take place, and why, and infuse a sense of spirituality into his design.

Sacred architecture includes structural patterns that reflect ancient traditions rooted in astrology, astronomy, the worship of deities and geometry, and is based on two primary shapes – the square and the circle. It is in the reconciliation of these shapes that sacred architecture emerges, symbolically 'squaring the circle' and representing the union of Heaven and Earth. The very earliest places of prayer were often a cube topped by a hemispheric cupola, to symbolize Heaven.

Christian Architecture

Traditionally, the footprint of Christian churches takes the form of a cross, the universal symbol of Christ and his crucifixion. They are topped by a cupola which symbolized the 'tent' of the world, the Heavens or celestial sphere. The church spire symbolizes God's finger pointing towards Heaven.

Cathedrals were built on strict geometric principles and the architects who built the early cathedrals wanted to create harmony in the perfect mathematical relations between height and width, which would inspire a sense of illumination and wonder in those who worshipped there. They strove to echo the sublime proportions of Heaven.

The early medieval Romanesque style of architecture was based on the Roman form of construction which emphasized security; each building was a fortress or stronghold and had a semi-defensive purpose. Romanesque style acts as the transition to Gothic architecture, which follows on from the Romanesque style.

There was a passion for pilgrimage in the Romanesque era; crusaders, monks and pilgrims travelled along set trails spurred on by stories of visions, miraculous cures and legends of the saints. This led to an upsurge of church-building to accommodate the spiritual needs of the pilgrims. The wide naves and broad transepts provided the space needed for large volumes of people to proceed towards the shrine. Chaucer describes a pilgrimage in *The Canterbury Tales* and the shrine to the Apostle James at Santiago de Compostela in Spain remains a popular pilgrimage route to this day.

The Cathedral of Santiago de Compostela is an example of a church built with a wide nave to accommodate increasing numbers of pilgrims.

ALTAR

The altar is a symbol of Christ's Last Supper, a place of physical and spiritual nourishment and the place where faith is reaffirmed. It represents sacrifice and the place where man and God connect in the act of Holy Communion, where the body and blood of Christ are symbolically taken by his followers.

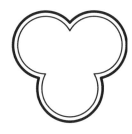

TREFOIL

The trefoil is the symbol of the Holy Trinity – Father, Son and Holy Spirit – and represents past, present and future.

TORCH OF TRUTH

Symbol of the Dominican order, this is often depicted being carried in the mouth of a small black dog. It is based on a dream that St Dominic's mother had when she was pregnant. Her child was a black-and-white dog bringing illumination to the world through the torch that was in his mouth.

QUATREFOIL

Quatrefoils have four leaves and were placed on churches to signify that the gospel, the bringer of peace and eternal life, was preached there.

THE PELICAN

This symbol of atonement and the Redeemer is found in church frescoes, murals, paintings and stained glass.

Gothic Architecture

The Romanesque gave way to the early Gothic in the middle of the 12th century, in which art, philosophy and religion combined to create some of the most dramatic sacred buildings. Perhaps the finest example of a medieval Gothic cathedral is Chartres Cathedral in France.

Gothic cathedrals consisted of flying buttresses, stone beams that extended from the walls, allowing rib-vaulted ceilings and more open interiors. People of the time saw these cathedrals as the Heavenly Jerusalem recreated on Earth, especially in the intricate stained-glass windows. The buildings let in more light than had been possible previously and appear to soar towards Heaven, with the enormous spires of the churches reaching even further.

Chartres Cathedral displays towering spires typical of Gothic architecture.

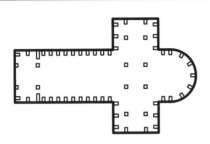

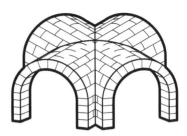

CRUCIFORM

The fundamental shapes found in all Gothic cathedrals were the cruciform or cross upon which its footprint was based, the octagonal baptism font and the circle, which is found throughout the structure, including in the magnificent circular rose windows.

VAULTING

Ribbed vaulting used columns to support the weight of the roof and gave an additional feeling of light and space, unlike the barrel vaulting of the Romanesque style.

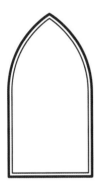

GOTHIC ARCH

In Gothic architecture, the new techniques of construction included pointed arches that enabled soaring ceilings to be raised, reflecting man's insignificance beneath the power of God.

ROSE WINDOWS

These magnificent structures reveal the love of the circle and geometric relationships. They work on three levels: the visual impact is manifest; the secret geometry of the relationship and proportion of parts is hidden, and there is also a symbolic level.

STAINED GLASS

Traditional sacred symbols in the artwork were included to help the worshipper understand the Church's teachings. The stained-glass windows often portray scenes from Christ's life.

STONE FRIEZES

The evangelists are often represented symbolically in stone friezes: St John by the eagle; St Mark by the lion; St Luke by the bull and St Matthew by a man. Also common is the Hand of God, emerging from clouds.

Islamic Architecture

As Islam forbids the use of and worship of religious images, so geometric form, colour and carefully proportioned design are the key features of Islamic sacred architecture. Aniconism – no representation of human or animal forms – and a doctrine of unity and harmony led to Islamic art being rich in geometric design, with the square and cube being used as repeat motifs.

Mecca is the most sacred site in Islam. All Muslim mosques face in its direction, as do worshippers when they pray. The square *Ka'aba* shape is repeated in square courtyards, which symbolize its stability. Eight angels support the Divine Throne, so Islamic mosques are often built onto an octagonal foundation, which can be aligned to the four cardinal points, the four intermediate points of Heaven and Earth.

Characteristically, mosques have large domes, tall towers and huge courtyards, all symbols of power. The repeated themes in geometric tile designs, calligraphy based on quotations from the Qur'an and arabesques symbolize Allah's infinite power. The domes represent the Heavens and creation. Muslims believe that Allah is to be found everywhere and so the whole world is a mosque.

The Dome of the Rock Mosque in Jerusalem (688–692 CE) is the oldest surviving example of Islamic sacred architecture. Made of marble and decorated with tile mosaics, it is topped by a dome covered in gold. It was built, not as a mosque for public worship, but as a *mashad*, a shrine for pilgrims.

The Dome is deeply significant as it is built on the rock on which Mohammed stood before he ascended to Heaven. It is also important to those who follow Judaism, as the rock symbolizes the foundation of the world.

The Royal Mosque or *Masjid-i-Shah* in Isfahan, built by Shah Abbas in the 17th century, is one of the most beautiful examples of sacred architecture in the world.

The dome of this mosque in Isfahan, Iran, is characteristically large and represents heaven.

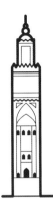

MINARET

The tall, graceful minarets found in mosques were originally lit by flaming torches and used as watchtowers. With their onion-shaped crowns, they represent spiritual illumination. The muezzin calls the faithful to prayer from the minaret and it is a permanent reminder of the presence of Allah. Like other towers, it symbolizes the link between humans on Earth and the Divine.

MIHRAB

The *mihrab* or niche is on the inside of the mosque and shows the direction of Mecca, towards which all Muslims must pray.

COURTYARD

Inside the courtyards of the mosque are fountains or water sources where the faithful wash before prayer. This literal and metaphorical cleansing represents the washing away of sin before presenting oneself to Allah.

Hindu Architecture

During the golden age of Indian architecture, the Gupta period in the 6th century CE, the *Vaastu Shastra* (*The Science of Building*) was written. This described construction methods, but was chiefly concerned with making buildings for gods and kings. It taught practitioners the way to create balance and harmony by using the subtle energies of people, buildings and the universe. Their sacred art is much more than the wise use of Earthly materials – it mediates between a higher, divine realm and also the human realm.

A Hindu temple, unlike a church or mosque, is where the gods live. Hindus do not use the temple to gather together and worship, rather they see it as a sculpture to be regarded from the outside. Devotees go in to make their offerings to the gods and then leave.

This Hindu temple in Chennai is decorated with figures of divine deities, which emphasize the sacred nature of the building.

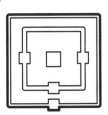

SQUARE

The fundamental form in Indian sacred architecture, the square is regarded as a perfect shape, a symbol of order. The temple should always face east because that is where the Sun appears and it represents the destruction of darkness. Also, only organic materials are used in the construction, because man-made materials are not regarded as good enough conductors of cosmic energy.

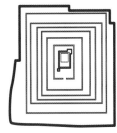

WALLS AND GATEWAYS

Sometimes seven concentric walls, *prakaras*, surround the temple, symbolizing the seven layers of matter: earth, water, fire, air, ether, mind and intelligence. The gateways or *gopurams* through the walls symbolize the release from the bonds of matter as the person goes towards the shrine at the centre of the temple.

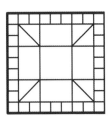

MANDALA

In India some architects use the ancient symbol of the mandala as the template for planning and designing buildings. Varanasi, alongside the sacred River Ganges, is India's most holy city and its design is based on the mandala.

FIGURES

Sculpted figures of divine deities are painted and carved into the temple to emphasize the sacred nature of the building.

HUMAN BODY SYMBOLISM

The temple is seen as being alive, like a human being, and different parts correspond to the human body. The door is the mouth, the dome is the head. The front pavilion or meeting room is the stomach, the walls surrounding it symbolize the legs, the *gopuram*, the tower of the entrance, represents the feet and the main image in the sanctum sanctorum or *Garbhagriha*, concealed in the darkness of the inner recess,

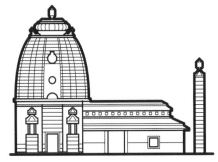

is the life force or *prana* in the body. Each part of the building symbolizes a limb of the god, so every section is sacred.

Buddhist Architecture

Early Buddhist sacred architecture sculpted buildings out of living rock, extracting materials from the earth or rock in order to form holy sites such as Ellora, northeast of Bombay. The Ajanta monastery (500–600 BCE) near Bombay was carved out of rock, as were many Buddhist monasteries of this time. Wooden columns and vault ribs were used to complete the internal structure. Later construction methods used the now-conventional method of adding materials to form the structures.

The caves at Ellora were carved out of rock and include 12 Buddhist temples.

STUPA

Stupas are large ceremonial mounds and buildings which contain Buddhist relics. The earliest were found in Nandangarth, India, and were royal burial mounds. After burial a wooden mast was placed in the centre to carry umbrellas which symbolized royalty and authority. In its simplest form, the stupa plan is a circle within a square.

The Hill of Sanchi at Madhaya Pradesh in India is a group of Buddhist monuments dating from about 250 BCE. Asoka (304–232 BCE), the first royal patron of the Buddha, built eight stupas over the remains of the Buddha, with two further stupas covering the urn and embers. Asoka also built free-standing monolithic columns, the most famous at Sarnath, which represented the connection between the Earth and Heaven.

The Temple of Borobodur in Java is made in the form of a lotus, the sacred flower of Buddha. For each direction there are 92 Buddhas placed in small stupas and each statue has a mudra, or hand gesture. The Borobodur represents the ten levels of a Bodhisattva's life, which a person must pass through in order to reach enlightenment.

PARASOL

The parasol is a symbol of Heaven and an emblem of kingship. It is also the emblem of the Buddha himself. The series of parasols on top of stupas and pagodas represent levels in the celestial world, the cosmic world and the world beyond man.

TRIRATNA/TRISULA

Also known as the *trisula*, the *triratna* is the symbol of the 'Three Jewels' of Buddha: the Buddha himself, Dharma or the teachings, and Sangha, the community who practise Buddhism. It often appears in carvings in venerated buildings.

POTALA PALACE

Potala Palace, which means 'Pure Land' is in Lhasa, Tibet, is an important place of pilgrimage for Buddhists. Completed in 1694, it rests on one of the highest points in the world and is covered in red, white and gold leaf. The golden-roofed monastery was the official home of the Dalai Lama, the spiritual leader of Tibetan Buddhism, and houses the tombs of previous Dalai Lamas. The current Dalai Lama has fled to northern India as a consequence of Chinese interference in all levels of Tibetan life.

FOOTPRINT OF THE BUDDHA

The footprint of the Buddha, *Buddhapada*, symbolizes Earth, the path of the Buddha and the journey towards enlightenment. It is carved or depicted in paintings in places he visited when he was alive and which are now venerated and are places of pilgrimage.

Taoist Architecture

Taoism keeps up ancient Chinese traditions of ritual worship of gods and the ancestors, who must be venerated in order to avoid any harm befalling human beings. Taoists believed in oracular prediction and veneration of the ancestors and the emperors.

In Taoism it is important to live simply in accord with the natural cycles of nature. Lao-tse instructed his followers to 'be still like a mountain and flow like a river'. Mountains were sacred to Taoists and so temples were set in sites of outstanding natural beauty. Sacred mountains are places of pilgrimage and monasteries are built on their slopes. The holiest peak is Tai Shan.

The Forbidden City in Beijing is built on a mandala, which symbolizes the emperor as the person who unites Heaven and Earth. Similarly, the Temple of Heaven is mandala-based, with four sub-mandala temples dedicated to the Earth, Moon, Sun and Heaven.

An offshoot of Taoism is feng shui, the art or science that determines how buildings are to be laid out so that the gods are appeased and the beneficial energy flow, *chi*, is maximized.

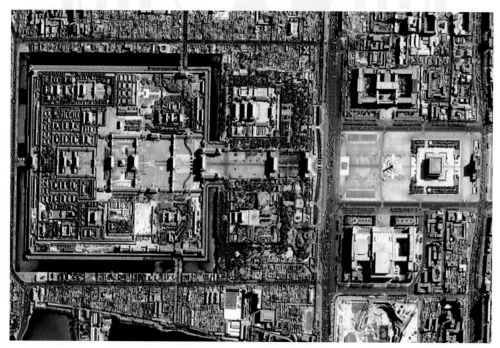

This view of the Forbidden City in Beijing shows clearly how its structure is based on a mandala.

PAGODAS

Originally Taoist pagodas were shrines or reliquaries attached to Buddhist temples.

In China, pagodas were usually placed at the entrance to a town in order to block access by evil spirits from the northeast, the direction of the devil. Pagodas were constructed of wood with an interlocking frame which enabled them to withstand earthquakes and typhoons.

The five-storey pagoda Horyuji in Nara, built 1,300 years ago, was recently added to the UNESCO

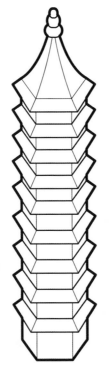

World Heritage list. Horyuji was the first Buddhist temple to be built in Japan and is the world's oldest wooden structure. It includes a pagoda or reliquary, a *kodo* or lecture hall and a *kondo* or image hall.

The pagoda often takes the form of a tower built over nine levels, symbolizing the nine levels of Heaven. In the Tang dynasty they were octagonal or diagonal. The pagoda is mainly used to house sacred objects. Pagoda temple roofs were curved to ward off evil spirits.

THE BAGUA (EIGHT TRIGRAMS)

Also written Pa Kua, this symbol arose in ancient China and symbolizes the beginning of the world. It is used in feng shui to locate or 'map' the home or building so that the most auspicious sites correlate with the given activity or purpose. The eight areas or *guas* of the Bagua surround a central motif. These areas correspond to prosperity, reputation, relationships, family, health, creativity, ability and knowledge, career and helpful people.

TIME, SHAPE, NUMBER AND COLOUR

Underpinning our lives are the fundamental concepts of shape, number, colour and time. They allow us to communicate, to build homes, to set up intricate internet systems and are the basis of everyday interactions. The earliest human drawings in existence are circles and spirals scratched on to the surface of stones, made by our earliest ancestors as they strove to leave their own mystical marks. A variety of geometrical figures also appear – dots, quadrants, chevrons and lines that seem to be cosmic symbols. Today we use highly complex systems of numerals, symbols and colour coding to manage the intricacies of 21st-century living.

Since the beginning of time, humanity has been surrounded by colour, the yellow Sun, the white Moon, the brown Earth, green foliage and the overarching blues of the day and night sky. Over millennia a whole system of colour interpretation developed and symbolic connections were made, which continue today. Our ancestors brightened their garments with vegetable dyes and ground pigments to paint on cave walls, paintings that venerated the animals they hunted.

Time

Our desire to measure time probably started as soon as we realized that the Sun moved across the sky and disappeared below the horizon, and with it came darkness. If man could measure time, it would give him some relief from the fear that the Sun might never rise again. By measuring time he could gain control over his world and plan his life more accurately.

THE EARLIEST CLOCK
The Moon was the earliest clock and ancestors noted its progress and recognized the coming of winter, the arrival of spring and other positions important to hunter-gatherers and, later, planters.

Almost all symbols of time have some relationship to the circle, whether the circular calendars of the Inca, the curved scythe or the astrological representation of the yearly cycle of the planets. Clock time chases itself like the Ouroboros swallowing its own tale and symbolizes the endless cycle of the life of the cosmos.

CALENDAR TIME
Calendar time, however, has fixed squares: once a day is over it will never come again. With calendar time we have past, present and future. The Gregorian calendar, used in the West, was the result of changes brought about by Pope Gregory XIII in 1582. It ensured that important religious festivals, such as Easter, were marked on the correct day. Not everyone agreed with the Catholic reform of the calendar, including Sweden, which finally adopted it in 1753.

The Moon was mankind's first timepiece, used by many different cultures.

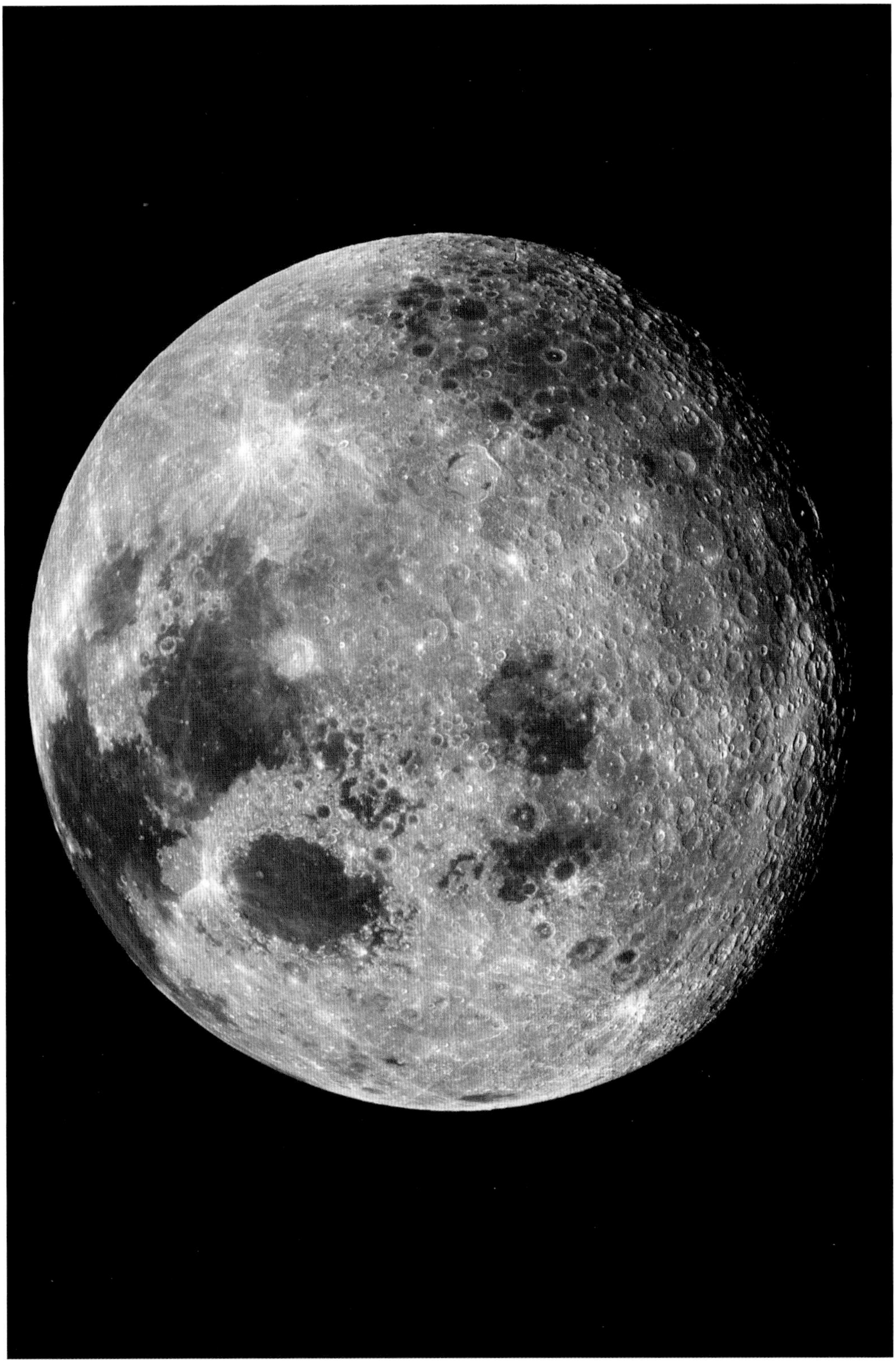

SCYTHE

The scythe is associated with death and the
planet Saturn. Cybele, goddess of nature and
fertility, the Great Mother goddess, was
worshipped in Rome by a cult controlled
by priests known as Corybantes, who staged
wild orgies in her honour. Cybele was linked
to self-harm or self-mutilation. All curved
objects such as the scythe are linked to
lunar and feminine practices. The scythe
expresses the hope of a fruitful harvest.
The contradictory symbolism of the scythe
in cutting down and bringing to an end
is consistent with the idea of sacrifice
and renewal.

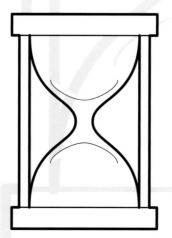

HOURGLASS

The hourglass symbolizes the upper and
lower worlds and the inversion of them.
The narrow opening between the two
sections represents the difficult task of
making that connection. It represents
creation and destruction, life and death.
The substance flowing from one part to the
other is like a river, and all rivers symbolize
time or the irreversible nature of processes
as they move onwards.

The sign for hour in 17th-century
French alchemy was two semi-circles
balanced on top of each other, the curved
parts facing each other. In modern times
the hourglass symbolizes time passing.

Death

Since humankind first told stories, a preoccupation with the end of life has manifested itself in the personification of death as a living character. Characters differ from society to society. These are two of the best known.

FATHER TIME

An old man carrying a scythe symbolizes death and the destroyer. The scythe originated with the Greek god of the harvest, Cronos, whose name was confused with the Greek prefix *chrono-*, pertaining to time. Father Time sometimes holds or rests his elbow on an hourglass, another symbol of death and passing time. He is depicted with a scythe, gathering in those whose hour of death has arrived.

GRIM REAPER

In Western cultures, death has long been seen as a skeletal figure, wearing a black gown with a hood and carrying a large scythe. The scythe is borrowed from the image of Father Time. The Grim Reaper's task is to gather the souls of the recently dead and guide them on into the afterlife.

Shape

The shapes that surround us carry archetypal meaning, and symbolize our cosmos and the world in which we live. The circle, perhaps the most profoundly significant of all shapes, is found everywhere in nature, while the square is man's own invention. The circle has celestial associations with the rainbow and represents the union of the Earthly and the divine.

The circle, square, crescent, triangle, cross and star are the foundations of mystical symbolism.

In traditions such as Judaism and Islam, where the likeness of God is not portrayed, abstract shapes are used to represent him.

The Round Table of King Arthur and his knights symbolizes equality.

SQUARE

To Pythagoras the square represented perfection. It stands for solidity and firmness and was an early symbol of the Earth, as opposed to the circle, which represented the Heavens. The square can be divided into two equal parts and these in turn can be divided into multiples of two. With an inscribed cross it is possible to divide it into eight triangles, which give the eight cardinal points, four cardinal directions and the four corners of the world.

In Egyptian hieroglyphs, the square denotes achievement. In Buddhism, the square or cube forms the base of the stupa, and represents the Earth level on the planes of existence. It is the basic template for Hindu temples or any sacred structure. The square is the archetype and pattern of order in the universe and the standard of proportion. The expression 'four-square' is a talismanic promise of stability and permanence.

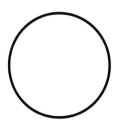

CIRCLE

The circle is a profound symbol found in all cultures and throughout all ages. It represents the Sun, without which there can be no life on Earth. It signifies wholeness, completeness, illumination, the cycle of life and rebirth, the wheel of life, the Philosopher's Stone of alchemy and, in many religious traditions, it is the all-seeing, all-knowing eye.

The circle is the most common symbol and has universal significance. It may have been the first shape drawn by humans, influenced as they were by the Sun. It has no beginning or end and so is a universal symbol of eternity, perfection, divinity, infinity, completion and the ultimate cosmic order. It symbolizes cycles of our natural world. The circle represents unity and is the preferred shape to signify equality, as exemplified in the Round Table of King Arthur, the Council Circle and the United Nations Assembly.

The circle is often depicted as a dragon or snake swallowing its own tail, devouring itself and being reborn. It symbolizes eternity and the endless cycle of change. The cross within a circle, found in many religious paintings, is taken as an example of squaring the circle.

In the form of a wheel, the circle symbolizes movement. The Wheel of Dharma, a Buddhist symbol, represents the teachings of the Buddha which continue to spread unceasingly. The Tibetan prayer wheel contains a prayer written on a piece of paper contained within the cylinder; when the wheel is turned it spins an endless prayer. As the wheel can turn, it has been associated with chance. The Wheel of Fortune symbolizes this aspect of the circle.

Carl Jung believed that the circle symbolizes the process of nature, the cosmos and the cycles of the universe, while the square represents the universe as man conceives and projects it.

The wedding ring is a symbol of unending love and is placed on the finger associated with the heart.

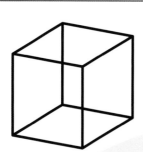

CUBE

As the cube cannot be rotated it symbolizes absolute stability and the Earth. A square in three dimensions, each face identical to the other, it represents truth because from whichever point you view it, it is always the same. It was used as a base in the Maya Tree of Life.

In Islam and Judaism the cube represents the centre of faith, which is seen particularly in the *Ka'aba*, a double cube, at the holiest of shrines, Mecca.

LABYRINTH

The labyrinth is a complicated series of paths in which it is difficult to find the centre or to find an exit. In Greek mythology, Daedalus built a labyrinth to imprison the Minotaur. The earliest labyrinths were found in Egyptian tombs and were built to foil tomb raiders. The labyrinth symbolizes the journey to the centre, the knowledge of God or self-knowledge. In some churches labyrinths are created on the floor or in the grounds, and followers walk the labyrinth as a symbol of pilgrimage.

SPIRAL

The spiral is one of the most ancient symbols. The basic elements of the dot and spiral were in use 24,000 years ago, but following that, the first examples, carved into rock faces, appeared about 5,000 years ago. It is found on stones from ancient Crete and, with minor variations, in Tibet where it was a symbol of potential power.

In Western symbolism, the clockwise spiral is associated with water, power and movement and with the migration of people. In Celtic symbolism, a single spiral symbolized growth, expansion and cosmic energy. To the ancient Irish, it symbolized the Sun. A loosely wound spiral in an anti-clockwise form represented the full summer Sun, while a closely wound clockwise spiral symbolized the contracting winter Sun. A double spiral represented the equinoxes when day and night are of equal length. Dual-centred spirals, like the yin-yang symbol, represent the duality of nature and balance.

A spiral with a triple centre, but emerging from a single point, symbolized the Trinity for early Christian monks who decorated their illuminated manuscripts with spirals.

Spirals were seen later in the borders of knotted carpets, on woven tapestries and on printed cloth. These were believed to have mystical powers of protection.

ZIGZAG

A primal geometric shape, the zigzag has numerous symbolic meanings. The ancient Babylonians saw it as the symbol of lightning, fire from lightning and fertility and it was associated with the storm gods. The god Adad is depicted holding a zigzag or three flames in his hand.

In Pech del'Aze, France, a piece of bone dating back 300,000 years was found inscribed with a zigzag which may symbolize water or snakes. Ancient Egyptians used a zigzag hieroglyph to represent water and it can also be seen in the symbol of the zodiac sign Aquarius. In the Norse Runic alphabet the letter 'S' takes the shape of a zigzag, a lightning flash; the sign for danger in modern times, especially near electricity pylons, is a sharpened zigzag.

CROSS

The cross is an archetypal symbol. It represents the world axis, the *axis mundi*, the great pole around which the constellations of the zodiac revolve. Situated in the mystic centre of the cosmos, it becomes a means by which the human soul can reach God. Jacob's ladder represents this connection. The Tree of Life is also a symbol of this link between Heaven and Earth, the sacred and the mundane.

It is a combination of two different signs, the vertical axis, the upright pole or symbolic ladder, and the horizontal crosspiece, which signifies the conjunction of opposites. In this sense the cross indicates the dual nature of Earthly or temporal concerns and our spiritual nature.

There are hundreds of varieties, and the cross signifies the conjunction of two worlds. It is found on tombstones and flags worldwide and relates to the marrying of physical and spiritual, the synthesis of active and passive.

Sacred Geometry

Geometry means 'earth measure' and originated in Egypt with the rope stretchers who each year marked out territory around the Nile after the annual inundation and used a rope triangle to make their calculations. This activity was also symbolic since it restored order on Earth and remade boundaries after the chaos brought by the floods. In this way geometry becomes sacred because it represents order.

Sacred geometry has had a special place in mysticism through the ages. It is based on measuring and counting. In earliest times this knowledge had mystical associations, since the priests who studied the skies in order to understand the influence of the Heavens on humanity kept their knowledge secret. Geometry became a symbolic system and included astronomy and astrology. It was studied by the priests of ancient Egypt, Babylon, Armenia, India, China and by the Incas and Maya of South America.

In sacred geometry, shapes and numbers are brought together to create harmonious structures which could unite humans with the cosmos. The shapes of the circle and square provide the basic building blocks. The principles of sacred geometry are manifest through proportions, shapes or symmetries considered to have special significance.

Karahundge, possibly the oldest known observatory in the world, is sited in Armenia and was built around 4200 BCE. The early Armenians had a sophisticated knowledge of astronomy and could predict astral events to a high degree of accuracy. They could measure distances, latitudes and longitudes, realized that the world was round and predicted solar and lunar eclipses millennia before the ancient Egyptians could do the same. The excavation of early fortress cities and temples in Armenia shows the use of sacred geometry, and complex buildings were made using squares, rectangles, circles and polygons with intersecting patterns.

The geometric symbols represent man's desire to understand the universe and to replicate it in symbolic form. Squaring the circle, forming a union with the two most important shapes, symbolized the reconciliation of the Heavenly and infinite with the Earthly and that which is made by man. The priests and mathematicians who worked out how to square the circle believed this would impress the cosmic forces that control life and would lead to more auspicious conditions on Earth. The mandala is an example of squaring the circle. In Sanskrit, *mandala* literally means centre or Holy Circle. Pyramids square the circle and reconcile triangle and square. *Vitruvian Man*, Leonardo da Vinci's famous drawing, is literally a man inside a square and a circle.

The spiral of the nautilus sea shell is a beautiful example of the Fibonacci sequence in nature.

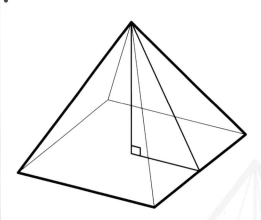

GOLDEN RATIO

The golden ratio is also known as Divine Proportion and is symbolized by the ratio 1:1.618. It has been used in designing buildings and artwork in many different cultures and is found in sacred architecture, the paintings of Leonardo da Vinci, city layouts and the pyramids in Eygpt. Many artists and architects have proportioned their works to approximate the golden ratio – especially in the form of the golden rectangle, in which the ratio of the longer side to the shorter is the golden ratio – believing this proportion to be aesthetically pleasing. The golden ratio also appears in nature, and mathematicians have studied it because of its unique and interesting properties.

GOLDEN MEAN

The golden section, golden mean or golden ratio is closely related to the Fibonacci sequence. It is normally denoted by the Greek symbol *phi* and is an integral part of design, since the proportion it produces creates harmonious structures which satisfy both eye and spirit. The Parthenon in Athens is the most famous example of the use of the golden section in architecture.

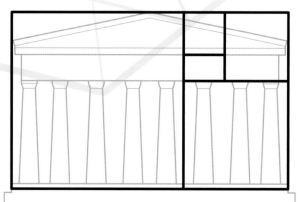

THE FIBONACCI SEQUENCE

Leonardo de Pisa, known as Fibonacci, travelled throughout the ancient world and returned to his home in Italy to write *Liber Abaci* (*The Book of Calculations*). He developed a sequence of numbers that begin with zero and one, then the last two numbers are added together to get the next number: 1, 2, 3, 5, 8, 13, 21, 34, 55, 89, 144...

Many plants and animals develop in accordance with this series, including the spiral of the nautilus sea shell. Plants such as sunflowers, daisies and pine cones also share this code. They have a Fibonacci number of growing points which can be clearly identified.

The sunflower reveals the Fibonacci code in its growing points.

Number

The greatest thinkers of Babylon, Sumeria and ancient Greece believed that numbers were the key to the mysteries of the cosmos. They thought that numbers could reveal the secrets of creation as well as the rules that controlled space and the laws of time. Medieval scholars believed the mathematical aspects of number to be of divine origin and that these sacred numbers had mystical powers.

PYTHAGORAS' OBSERVATION OF THE SKIES

The philosophy of Pythagoras (*c.*582–507 BCE) rests on the understanding that numbers rule the universe. It is based on observation of the stars and planets, geometric shapes or anything from which a ratio could be derived. Pythagoras worked with the duality of odd and even numbers, which symbolized the finite and the infinite. Even numbers represented the feminine principle and cyclical movement, while odd numbers represented the male principle and fixed positions.

SACRED NUMBERS

Sacred numerology included not only the numbers themselves but their combinations. 18 (1+8) gives 9, a sacred number that is used in sacred geometry, so a building may have nine steps leading to the entrance, and nine sets of intersecting triangles to draw the eye towards Heaven or a religious icon that is displayed in the building.

In the Bible, support was found for the importance of numbers. In the 'Wisdom of Solomon' it says, 'But thou hast arranged all things by measure, and number and weight', and for medieval man , trying to make sense of the world, geometry became a divinely inspired pursuit. Churches were built on geometric principles, as were ancient temples.

In the Forbidden City in Beijing, the number of animals decorating a roof denoted the importance of the building or the inhabitant. The number nine was associated with the Emperor and was found throughout the complex.

I ONE

One represents unity and wholeness, the first and only. It has no divisors and no factors and stands independently. It represents harmony and peace. In Christian symbolism, one stands for the undivided Oneness of God. It symbolizes the god or deity since it is also part of all numbers. It represents the beginning and creation. The single menhir or standing stone, the rod or staff and the erect phallus reflect this sense of primal creation.

II TWO

Two represents polarity, the realm of opposites and diversity. In Christian symbolism it signifies the two aspects of Christ, the divine and the human. Two is also seen in yin-yang, Sun and Moon, good and evil, night and day, man and woman. The duality can be seen in the Greek god Janus, whose name gave us January. He is depicted facing backwards and forwards and sees both ways.

Guardian figures are traditionally made in pairs because they double the sense of protection from threat. Symmetry and repetition are powerful elements in magic-protective symbolism; for example, pairs of ceramic lions are seen as bringers of good fortune in China, and were used to decorate the entrances to temples and palaces.

III THREE

Three is a holy number. It represents the Trinity in Christian faith – Father, Son and Holy Spirit; it also represents the three Wise Men or Magi. In India the three Hindu deities are Brahma, Vishnu and Shiva; and Babylon had Anu, Bel and Ena, representing Heaven, Earth and the abyss. The ancient Egyptians divided the Sun god into three deities: Horus, the rising Sun, Re or Ra, the midday Sun, and Osiris, the setting Sun. There are three divisions of time: past, present and future; and three kingdoms of matter: animal, vegetable and mineral.

IV FOUR

Four represents solidity and material things and is associated with the Earth. In Christian symbolism there are the four main prophets, the four evangelists and the four gospels. There are the four cardinal points, identified with four directions, towards sunrise, towards the sunset and the two directions perpendicular to them, giving north, south, east and west. And the four humours of the body, the four seasons, the four stages in man's life, the four cardinal virtues, as well as the four phases of the moon. In numerology the cross is sometimes represented by the number four.

Within the Rosicrucian tradition four is a mystic number and relates to the power of the four elements. It was with this number, or the 'geometric square' that Pythagoras communicated the ineffable Name of God to his chosen followers. The Divine Quadernity was familiar to those who followed Hermetic philosophy of the Middle Ages. The Hindu Vedas are divided into four sections. The universe is based on four elements – earth, air, water and fire.

V FIVE

Five consists of two unequal parts, three and two, which symbolizes disruption. Five fingers and five toes and the five senses: taste, touch, sight, smell and hearing.

In Christian symbolism it represents the five wounds of Christ. The Pythagorean brotherhood used the pentagram as a symbol of their school. A pentagram within a circle symbolizes the human form, the five points representing the head, two arms and two legs, while the circle signifies the Earth. Rosicrucian teachings say that five is the emblem of health and safety and represents the spirit plus the four elements.

Five was important in the Celtic tradition: Ireland had five main roads, five provinces and five paths of the law. The fairies were believed to count in fives, and mythical figures had fivefold cloaks which could make them invisible. Mars is the planet associated with five.

VI SIX

Six is the sum of three plus three and is regarded as perfect. According to Genesis, God created the Earth in six days and included the four points of the compass plus the nadir and zenith. Six is the powerful symbol of mystical destiny depicted in six equilateral triangles contained in a circle. It is a power that can be used for good or evil. In China six is the number of Heaven, celestial power and long life.

In the West, the six-pointed star became the emblem of Israel, the Seal of Solomon or the Star of David and, as a pair of inverted triangles, signifies the union of opposites.

The Maya dedicated the sixth day to their rain god and regarded six as an unlucky number.

VIII EIGHT

In Buddhism the sacred eight-spoked wheel represents the eightfold path to spiritual enlightenment. In Taoism there are Eight Immortals and Eight Emblems (see pages 106–107). In Christian symbolism eight is the symbol of regeneration, of new life after baptism, and many baptismal fonts are in the shape of an octagon.

VII SEVEN

Seven is a magical number associated with celestial beings and mystical forces. In ancient times there were only seven known planets: the Sun, Moon, Mercury, Venus, Mars, Jupiter and Saturn. We have seven days of the week and the seven levels of a ziggurat.

On the seventh day, God rested after creating the world, in Christian symbolism. The Sabbath was a covenant with Adam, and there were seven colours of the rainbow, the symbol of the covenant God made with Noah after the flood. Noah was instructed to take seven pairs of clean beasts and given seven days to prepare for the flood. There are seven sacraments, seven virtues and seven vices.

Seven symbolizes triumph and victory. There are seven main chakras in the body. In ancient Egypt there were seven gods of light and seven gods of darkness. In Islam there are seven Heavens, seven Hells and seven Earths.

Seven is a favoured number in Judaism. There are seven days in the Jewish Passover and seven branches of the Menorah. The acts of atonement and purification were accompanied by a sevenfold sprinkling. In Persian mythology, the hero Rustam performed seven superhuman labours to save the life of his father Zal.

NINE

In China, nine is seen as being a particularly lucky number and symbolizes the number of celestial spheres. The cat has nine lives, symbolizing its ability to avoid death, which may be why a black cat was known as a witch's familiar. In Christian terms, nine represents man's imperfection and the choir of angels. The result of three multiplied by three makes nine an even holier number than three.

TEN

Ten is the round and perfect number that provides the basis for the decimal system; to Pythagoras it was the universal divine number. St Augustine described ten as the perfect number because it is the sum of three plus seven. It is found in the Ten Commandments, which give three laws related to the love of God and seven to the love of one's neighbour. In the Jewish tradition it is seen in the ten ropes of the tent of the Tabernacle and the ten horns of the apocryphal beast.

ELEVEN

Eleven is viewed as a negative number as it exceeds the perfection of ten. It is a symbol of transition, conflict and excess. In numerology eleven is 1 + 1, which gives the number two, which represents balance.

TWELVE

The number twelve formed the basis of the Sumerian and Babylonian numerical system. In ancient Egypt, twelve was the number of provinces of the Underworld.

We have the twelve houses of the zodiac, twelve months of the year, twelve hours in a day and, in the Jewish faith, the twelve tribes of Israel, the twelve bronze calves and the twelve gates of paradise. And in Christian symbolism, the twelve Apostles of Christ and twelve gates to Jerusalem.

The rose window, found in Christian cathedrals and churches, is traditionally divided into twelve segments. Some say this is because of the influence of astrology. In Chartres Cathedral, famous for its three large rose windows, there are zodiac signs over the west doorway and a zodiac window.

THIRTEEN

Often thirteen is seen as an unlucky number. There were thirteen at the Last Supper, so it represents betrayal and Judas Iscariot. The Kabbalah has thirteen spirits of evil.

Colour

Ancient civilizations invested colour with mystical power and honoured it as a manifestation of the light of their gods. Rainbows, which revealed all the colours of the visible spectrum, were seen as Heaven-sent and the bridge between the celestial world above and Earthly world below.

We depend on light for our existence. Without the life-giving force of the Sun we would have no plants to provide food, no trees to provide shelter and take up toxic gas and provide oxygen, and without light and the reassuring glow of the Moon and stars we would have only the darkness of unending night. Science has shown that colour influences our mood and early man was aware of the differences between colours on a symbolic level – they saw that certain colours were reassuring while others repelled. They 'read' the reactions of animals and birds to natural colours, their own feeling responses to colours, and so a symbolism of colours came into existence.

Colour stirs our emotions and hits the brain faster than speech or the written word. As symbolic systems evolved in sacred architecture, in the paintings of icons, the tinctures of heraldry and those associated with royalty and authority colour played a pivotal role in making those mystical symbols work at a very deep level.

Each energy centre or chakra in the body is associated with a particular colour.

The rainbow symbolizes the connection between Heaven and Earth.

RED

Red is the first colour of the rainbow so it takes a prime position. Red is the colour of blood, heat, power, passion and danger. Many cultures see it as energizing and stimulating. The base chakra is red and it contains our primal energy, the *Kundalini Shakti*.

Red is a lucky colour throughout Asia because it symbolizes the life force. Red is also the colour of power. In medieval times the wearing of red coats was the exclusive right of the nobility. It is also linked to blood sacrifice in esoteric rituals and feuds. In the Middle Ages red-haired women were reputed to be witches and whores, and the poppy was known as the devil's flower. As Christianity grew, red was associated with lust and uncontrolled licentiousness and was viewed with disfavour.

Red is the colour of danger: red traffic lights call for us to stop and emergency buttons are usually red. In more recent times red was the colour of Communism. Spanish bullfighters use red capes to taunt bulls, and red is the colour of the 'red-faced' person who is angry or embarrassed. When we lose control we 'see red' or the 'red mist' descends.

Buddhists call red the colour of activity and creativity. In the Christian tradition red is the colour of blood and is the liturgical colour for the commemoration of martyred saints and fire. It is used at Pentecost.

BLUE

The colour of the sky and sea, blue symbolizes spaciousness, eternity and spirituality.

The throat chakra, symbolized by a blue lotus, acts as a channel between heart and mind. The ancient Egyptians used blue to represent truth, while the ancient Greeks associated blue with Zeus and Hera, the gods of Heaven, and with Aphrodite, the goddess of love. It is the colour of the Archangel Michael, and the bodies of the Hindu gods Krishna and Vishnu are depicted in vibrant blue to highlight their divinity.

Royal blue was the colour of King David, the most important leader of the Jewish people. The shade of blue is also the colour of Nut, the Egyptian goddess of night, who represents wisdom. Blue is the colour associated with Kwan Yin, Eastern goddess of Mercy, Hera and Mary, mother of Jesus. Their blue robes symbolize their Heavenly connection as well as eternal devotion and spiritual wisdom.

Blue symbolizes loyalty, devotion, friendship and truth and many military forces have blue uniforms to instil trust in the wider world. In heraldry, coats of arms have used 'azure' to symbolize piety and sincerity.

GREEN

Green is the colour of the goddess Venus and of nature at her most fertile. It symbolizes hope, renewal and rebirth. Green is the colour of the heart chakra, which is the centre of love and harmony. The Egyptian *Book of the Dead* calls for a green scarab stone to be placed on the chest of the deceased to 'open his mouth' so that he could communicate in the afterlife. The ancient Egyptians depicted Osiris, god of vegetation, as green to represent the fertility of nature.

In Islam, green is a sacred colour as it represents fertility in arid desert regions and knowledge. Those who go to Paradise after death wear green robes. In the West, it is the symbol of hope after winter darkness, and the first shoots of spring represent regeneration and the start of a new life cycle. Green symbolizes the deep and hidden knowledge that nature conceals. In China, it corresponds to the trigram *ch'en*, the 'arousing', the manifestation of springtime, thunder and the beginning of the ascendancy of yang.

Alchemists believe that emerald light could access the most deeply guarded secrets and so green is associated with occult mysteries. In the Christian tradition, green symbolizes the triumph of life over death and is the liturgical colour during the Epiphany and for the Sundays after Pentecost.

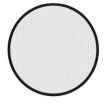

YELLOW

Yellow is the colour of the Sun at its most intense and associated with Athena, goddess of wisdom and patroness of learning and the arts. Her robes were golden. The solar plexus chakra is yellow, the brightest colour of the spectrum and is associated with learning, creativity and psychic energy.

In China, yellow is the colour sacred to the emperor and of the Sun. Saffron is the colour associated with Hinduism. Buddhist and Hindu monks and nuns wear robes of this colour to signify their renunciation of the material life.

PURPLE

In ancient Rome only the emperor was allowed to wear purple robes. It was prohibitively expensive to achieve the colour purple before chemical dyes were invented. 'Born to the purple' signified royal birth, and in heraldry purple or 'murrey' indicates royalty or high rank.

Ulysses wore purple robes on his mythical journey recorded in the *Odyssey*. They symbolize triumph over danger. The ancient Egyptians wore purple amulets to ward off adversity.

The crown chakra, which connects to the Universal spirit, is purple.

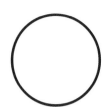

WHITE

White has been the symbol of celebration since Roman times. It represents purity and virginity and is used in the Christian liturgy during Christmas and Easter. In the East, it is the colour of mourning – Hindu widows wear white as a sign of their loss.

Australian Aborigines use white to depict the world of spirits. They surround the human forms they draw with heavy white lines, indicating that the spirit world begins just outside the human body. White is the colour of light and, usually regarded as a lucky colour. In Morocco when a couple are betrothed, milk is drunk to symbolize a 'white' or lucky life.

BLACK

Black indicates the absence of light and signals the power of darkness. It is a sign of mourning in much of Islam and in the Christian West. Black magic is associated with harm and malign forces.

In ancient Egypt black was the sign of resurrection from the dead and eternal life. It was also the colour of the god Anubis, who took the dead into the Underworld, and of the god Min, who controlled growth and harvest.

In the Christian tradition black is generally associated with penance. In Africa black is the colour of the night, pain, adversity as well as mystery. In Islam it is an unlucky colour: a black dog is said to bring death to the family, black hens were used in witchcraft and black is used as a charm against the evil eye. Mystics describe black as the colour of divine essence since it contains all colours and makes them indistinguishable, hence it is the symbol of undivided oneness. The veil of the *Ka'aba* is black.

Bibliography

Askews, M. 2001, *Guide to Astrology*, Caxton Editions, London

Barrie, T., 1996, *Spiritual Path, Sacred Space: Myth, Ritual and Meaning in Architecture*, Shambhala, Boston

Bazin, G., 1958, *Concise History of Art*, Thames & Hudson, London

Beer, R., 1999, *The Encyclopedia of Tibetan Symbols and Motifs*, Shambhala, Boston

Berg, Y., 1988, *The Power of Kabbalah*, Hodder-Mobius, London

Binder, P., 1972, *Magic Symbols of the World*, Hamlyn, London

Bloom, W., 1998, *Working with Angels, Fairies & Nature Spirits*, Piatkus, London

Brody, H., 1982, *Maps and Dreams*, Pantheon Books, New York

Brunton, P., 1977, *A Search in Secret Egypt*, Samuel Weisler, Inc., Maine, USA

Buckland, R., 2003, *Signs, Symbols & Omens*, Llewellyn Publications, St Paul, Minnesota

Bursten, D.,(Ed.) 2004, *Secrets of the Code*, Weidenfeld & Nicolson, London

Campbell, J. & Moyers, B., 1988, *The Power of Myth*, Doubleday, New York

Chevalier, J. & Gheerbrandt, A., 1996, *The Penguin Dictionary of Symbols*, Penguin Books, London

Cirlot, J.E., *A Dictionary of Symbols*, Routledge & Kegan Paul, London

Clark, K., 1969, *Civilization*, Harper and Row, New York

Clarke, P. B., 1993, *The World's Religions*, Reader's Digest Association, London

Cooper, J.C., 1977, *The Symbolism of the Taoist Garden*, Studies in Comparative Religion

Cooper, J.C., 1998, *An Illustrated Encyclopaedia of Traditional Symbols*, Thames & Hudson, London

Cooper, R.L.D., 2006, *Cracking The Freemason's Code*, Rider, London

Craze, R., 1997, *Feng Shui*, Hodder & Stoughton, London

Critchlow, K., 1969, *Order in Space*, Thames and Hudson, London

Crowley, A., 1976, *Magick in Theory and Practice*, Dover, New York

Drury, N. 2005, *The Watkins Dictionary of Magic*, Watkins Publishing, London

Duncan, D.E., 1998, *The Calendar*, Fourth Estate, London

Eisler, Riane, 1987, *The Chalice and the Blade: Our History, Our Future.* HarperCollins, New York

Eliade, M., 1962, *The Forge and the Crucible*, University of Chicago Press, Chicago

Etienne, R. & F., 1992, *The Search for Ancient Greece*, Thames & Hudson, London

Ettinghausen, R. & Grabar, O., 1994, *The Art and Architecture of Islam 650 – 1250*, Yale University Press

Fontana, D., 2003, *The Secret Language of Symbols*, Chronicle Books, San Francisco

Frazer, J.G., 1960, *The Golden Bough*, A Study in Magic and Religion, Macmillan, London

Gallagher, A-M., 2005, *The Wicca Bible*, Godsfield Press, London

Starhawk, 1999, *The Spiral Dance: A rebirth of the ancient religion of the great goddess*, HarperSanFrancisco

Gifford, J., 2000, *The Celtic Wisdom of Trees*, Godsfield Press, London

Glancey, J., 2000, *The Story of Architecture*, Dorling Kindersley, London

Gibson, C., 2006, *The Hidden Life of Art*, Saraband, Glasgow

Gombrich, E.H., 1966, *The Story of Art*, Phaidon, London

Graves, R., 1948, *The White Goddess*, Farrer, Strauss & Giroux, New York

Hall, N., 1980, *The Moon and the Virgin*, Women's Press, London

Harding, M., 1999, *A Little Book of the Green Man*, Aurum Press Ltd, London

Hillman, J., 1996, *The Souls's Code*, Bantam Books, London

Ions, V., 1978, *The World's Mythology*, Hamlyn, London

Jean, G., 2000, *Writing: The Story of Alphabets and Scripts*, Thames and Hudson, London

Jean, G., 2004, *Signs, Symbols and Ciphers: Decoding the Message*, Thames & Hudson, London

Jung, C.G., 1964, *Man and His Symbols*, Aldus Books, London

Jung, C.G., 1968, *The Archetypes and the Collective Unconscious*, Routledge, London

Kee, R., 1980, *Ireland: A History*, Weidenfeld & Nicolson, London

Lau, D.C. 1963, *Lao-Tzu: Tao Te Ching*, Penguin, London

Lloyd, G.E.R., 2002, *The Ambitions of Curiosity*, Cambridge University Press, Cambridge

Magnusson, M., 1976, *Hammer of the North*, Orbis, London

Mallon, B., 2003, *The Dream Bible*, Godsfield Press, Arlesford, UK

Mallon, B., 2001, *Venus Dreaming*, Newleaf, Gill & MacMillan, Dublin

Mallon, B., 2002, *Creative Visualization with Colour*, Vega, London

Mann, A.T., 2002, *Sacred Architecture*, Vega Books, London

Nuttgens, P., 1997, *The Story of Architecture*, Phaidon, London

O'Connell M. & Airey, R., 2005, *The Illustrated Encyclopedia of Signs & Symbols*, Lorenz Books, London

O'Murchu, D. 1998, *Reclaiming Spirituality: A New Spiritual Framework for Today's World*, Crossroad
    Pub. Co., New York

Paxton, J. & Fairfield, S., 1982, *Calendar of Creative Man*, MacMillan Press Ltd., London

Piggott, J., 1982, *Japanese Mythology*, Hamlyn, London

Roland, P., 2000, *New Age Living*, Hamlyn, London

Russell, J.B., 1980, *A History of Witchcraft*, Thames and Hudson, London

Saini, B., 2000, *Ancient Symbols in Architecture, Architecture+Design, VolXVII, No. 4*, New Delhi

Seignobos, C., 1975, *The World of Babylon*, Editions Minerva, S.A., Geneve

Shepherd, R. & R., 2002, *1000 Symbols; What shapes mean in art & myth*, Thames & Hudson, London

Snyder, G.F., 2003, *Ante Pacem: Archeological Evidence of Church Life Before Constantine*, Mercer
    University Press, Macon, Georgia

Sommer, D., 1995, *Chinese religion: An Anthology of Sources*, Oxford University Press, Oxford

Stewart, W., 1998, *Dictionary of Images and Symbols in Counselling*, Jessica Kingsley Publishers, London

Sullivan, M. 1962, *The Birth of Landscape Painting in China*, Routledge & Kegan Paul, London

Temple, R., 1990, *Icons and the Mystical Origins of Christianity*, Element, Shaftesbury, Dorset

Tompkins, P., 1971, *Secrets of the Great Pyramid*, Harper and Row, New York

Tressider, J., (Ed), 2004, *The Complete Dictionary of Symbols*, Duncan Baird Publishers, London

Turville-Petre, E.O.G., 1964, *Myth and Religion of the North: The Religion of Ancient Scandinavia*,
    Weidenfeld and Nicholson, London

Van de Weyer, R., 1990, *Celtic Fire*, Darton, Longman and Todd Ltd, London

Von Franz, M-L., 1995, *Creation Myths*, Shambala, Boston

Waite, A.E., 2002, *The Book of Ceremonial Magic*, Lethe Press

Walker, B.G., 1988, *The Woman's Dictionary of Symbols and Sacred Objects*, HarperCollins,
    San Francisco

Waterlow, J., 1994, *Looking Into The Past: The Ancient Chinese*, Thomson, New York

Wells, D., 1997, *100 Flowers*, Algonquin Books of Chapel Hill, North Carolina

Wood, J., 2000, *The Celtic Book of Living and Dying*, Duncan Baird Publishers, London

Zolar, 1972, *The History of Astrology*, Foulsham & Co. Ltd., Slough, England

Index

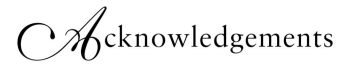Acknowledgements

Author acknowledgements
Thanks to Sandra Rigby for commissioning 'The Mystic Symbols' and to Lisa John for her joy and patience in editing the book. On the home front, my grateful thanks to Crystal and Danny for help with research and to Styx and the 'Early Doors' crew for making every Friday so special.

Commissioning Editor Sandra Rigby
Editor Lisa John
Senior Art Editor Sally Bond
Designer Cobalt ID
Production Manager Simone Nauerth
Illustrations Sudden Impact Media

AKG-images 133
Alamy/Eye Ubiquitous 234; /Eddie Gerald 101; /Colin Harris/LightTouch Images 177; /David Levenson 29; /Mary Evans Picture Library 16, 108; /Popperfoto 35; /Rolf Richardson 232
Bridgeman Art Library/British Library, London, UK 111
Corbis UK Ltd/Archivo Iconografico, S.A. 125; /Bettmann 223, 248; /Stefano Bianchetti 209; /Christie's Images 55; /Richard Cummins 39; /Ric Ergenbright 187; /Robert Gill/Papilio 21; /Darrell Gulin 49; /John Heseltine 228; /Historical Picture Archive 181; /Andrea Jemolo 230; /Bob Krist 8; /Ludovic Maisant 169; /Tatiana Markow/Sygma 66; /David Muench 242; /Jose Fuste Raga 257; /NASA/Roger Ressmeyer 245; /Sakamoto Photo Research Laboratory 206; /Keren Su 166; /Craig Tuttle 262; /Sandro Vannini 11; /Brian A. Vikander 90; /Adam Woolfitt 75
David Sanger Photography 200; /Don Smith 83
DigitalVision 255
Getty Images 253; /Walter Bibikow 236; / DigitalGlobe 240; /R H Productions 238
Photolibrary/Suzanne Friedrich 215
Photodisc 52, 61, 79, 80
TopFoto/The British Library/HIP 184; /Charles Walker 71, 161
Werner Forman Archive/National Museum of Anthropology, Mexico 44